Whose Torah?

Also by Rebecca Alpert

Exploring Judaism: A Reconstructionist Approach
(co-authored with Jacob Straub)

Lesbian Rabbis: The First Generation
(co-edited with Sue Levi Elwell and Shirley Idelson)

Like Bread on the Seder Plate

Voices of the Religious Left:
A Contemporary Sourcebook

Whose Torah?

A CONCISE GUIDE TO
PROGRESSIVE JUDAISM

Rebecca T. Alpert

THE NEW PRESS

NEW YORK
LONDON

Requests for permission to reproduce selections from this book should be
mailed to: Permissions Department, The New Press, 38 Greene Street,
New York, NY 10013.

Published in the United States by The New Press, New York, 2008
Distributed by W. W. Norton & Company, Inc., New York

LIBRARY OF CONGRESS CATALOGING-IN-PUBLICATION DATA

Alpert, Rebecca T. (Rebecca Trachtenberg) © 1950–
Whose Torah? : a concise guide to progressive Judaism / Rebecca T. Alpert.
        p.   cm.
Includes bibliographical references.
ISBN 978-1-59558-336-9 (hc.)
1. Judaism and social problems.   2. Social justice—Religious aspects—
Judaism.   3. Justice (Jewish theology).   4. Jewish ethics.   I. Title.
HN40.J5A56   2008
296.3'8—dc22   2007043903

The New Press was established in 1990 as a not-for-profit alternative to
the large, commercial publishing houses currently dominating the book
publishing industry. The New Press operates in the public interest rather
than for private gain, and is committed to publishing, in innovative ways,
works of educational, cultural, and community value that are often deemed
insufficiently profitable.

www.thenewpress.com

Composition by dix!
This book was set in New Caledonia

Printed in the United States of America

2   4   6   8   10   9   7   5   3   1

For Christie
in solidarity, indeed

Contents

Foreword
Elaine Pagels

I met Rebecca Alpert (then Trachtenberg) at Barnard College in 1970, the first year I began teaching after graduate school. Then a senior, Rebecca had just returned from her junior year abroad, and I was her advisor. She had chosen to write an undergraduate thesis about the adaptation of the Jewish people to the Roman destruction of the Second Temple—a thesis that won a prize. We came to know each other after she sat in on every course I taught that year. I encouraged her to go on to graduate studies and focus on the Jews of the Roman era, but she decided instead to become a rabbi and a student of contemporary Jewish life.

Yet we can see now that she never lost her interest in how the Jewish people adapt to changing circumstances. Since that time she has investigated key moments in modern American religious history, including the development of the pastoral counseling and Reconstructionist movements of the mid-twentieth century and the more recent emergence of lesbians and gay men as a force within the American Jewish community (not to mention her interest in the role Jews have played in baseball—but that's another story). She has gone on to become a leader not only in progressive Jewish circles but in the larger world of scholars who study religion.

In this book, she explores how progressives are reshaping American Judaism, and she is informed not only by her excellent scholarship but also by a lifetime of activism. Her commitments range from reproductive rights to peace in the Middle East. She writes, too, in a clear and accessible style that will interest those who know a lot about Jewish tradition as well as those who don't.

Rebecca offers us all crucial insights about Jews committed to justice and a better society and how they approach issues central to ethics and politics today. Those of us involved in other religious traditions—as well as those who participate in none—realize increasingly that to understand the twenty-first century, we need to understand more about religion, especially about progressive dimensions of religion.

Those who share these concerns will be glad, as I am, that we have as a resource this incisive, fascinating, and thought-provoking book.

Whose Torah?

Introduction

You learn a lot about people and groups from the jokes that they tell about themselves and the ones that are told about them. Perhaps you've heard the quip that goes if you meet two Jews you can be sure they have three opinions between them. Or the one about the Jew stranded on a desert island, who, when rescued, showed off two structures: "the synagogue I go to and the synagogue I don't go to."

You might assume that means that we're a quarrelsome people. On the contrary—we're actually a people who appreciate a good argument and who don't assume that there's only one authentic way to be Jewish or practice Judaism, although we probably disagree about that, too. Even the word we use for our most holy book, *Torah*, has several meanings. The word really translates as "teaching." It is used most often to refer to the first five books of the Hebrew Bible: Genesis, Exodus, Leviticus, Numbers, and Deuteronomy. That's usually what we mean when we say "the Torah." But it can also mean any text or lesson Jews might think has wisdom to share.

Still, it is fair to say that we aren't expected to rigidly adhere to doctrine dictating how we interpret and live out our faith, or our lack of it. Of course, the question of who gets to define Judaism, or how to interpret Torah, is one about which you'll find at least three opinions for every two Jews you meet.

One of the things Jews argue over is where progressive values fit in Jewish life today. For me, they've always been at the very heart of being Jewish. I didn't come from an observant family, but my lobster-eating aunt and uncle would put aside their *treif* (nonkosher) habits and make a traditional gefilte-fish-and-four-cup-of-wine Seder every Passover. I loved the food and the singing, but above all I was taken by the story. Jews believe in a God whose main interest was to take a bunch of rebellious slaves and set them free from oppression—who could top that?

Attending a Reform synagogue in Brooklyn in the early 1960s, I learned about the biblical prophets Micah, Isaiah, and Amos and their passion for feeding the hungry and protecting orphans. The prophets were central to one of Reform Judaism's main goals—using Jewish teachings to support the civil rights movement. When Jewish leaders marched in Selma, Alabama, with Martin Luther King Jr., I felt proud: this is what Jews do in the world—they strive to make it a better place.

I decided to become a rabbi as a way to commit my life to the progressive Jewish values I'd learned in my childhood. I could work against poverty and for freedom. Of course, things got more complicated. After 1967, Jewish priorities focused more on internal Jewish matters, mostly Israel and the Holocaust. But there were still many Jews who saw Judaism as a vehicle to change the world. For us, the saying of the ancient rabbi Hillel—"If I am not for myself, who will be for me, but if I am only for myself, what am I, and if not now, when?"—kept a progressive vision alive. Sure, Jews needed to care for ourselves and our community, but if we cared only for other Jews, what were we?

Working in the Jewish community, I had the opportunity to meet many Jews who shared my commitments to justice and peace. We worked to end the nuclear arms race in an upstart organization known as the Shalom Center. I joined Breira, a group working to support peace in the Middle East, in the 1970s, and in the 1980s New Jewish Agenda, a multi-issue progressive organization that was among the first to champion gay and lesbian rights. I became part of a synagogue, Mishkan Shalom (Sanctuary of Peace), that took its name from the movement to provide sanctuary to refugees from Central America fleeing repressive regimes supported by the U.S. government.

Being a rabbi meant that I had clout, and I used my status to speak out at rallies and demonstrations against the death penalty or in favor of abortion rights. I got to travel to Haiti on a rabbinic mission in support of democracy there. I wrote about these issues in journals such as *Bridges* and *Menorah* and the *Reconstructionist.* I got to teach about the Jewish ethics of health care, social justice, gender, and how the Holocaust and slavery frame Jewish and Black experiences of oppression. But, of course, my approach to Judaism wasn't universally embraced in the Jewish community. I often had the feeling that if I met up with the Jew stranded on the desert island, he might build another synagogue just for me and my progressive friends.

Often this disagreement takes the form of a debate over who belongs in the Jewish tent to begin with. Who gets to claim it's *their* Judaism depends on where we come down on the troublesome question of who is a Jew. This was not always such a contentious matter. For a very long time, the definition was clear. You were a Jew if you either were born of a Jewish mother or went through a ceremony of conversion, although the latter was not all that common. Not too many people wanted to be Jewish when being Jewish meant being persecuted, as it often did in the past. The Nazis complicated things when they designated anyone with even one (or later two) Jewish grandparent as a Jew. The establishment of the State of Israel in 1948 made defining Jewish belonging more important, as the founders granted automatic Israeli citizenship to anyone who could demonstrate Jewish identity. Now, in these times of relative comfort and acceptance, Jews frequently marry outside the faith and their partners (and extended families) are attracted to becoming involved in Judaism, sometimes without benefit of conversion. As more people claim the label "Jew" there is more disagreement about who belongs and who doesn't.

Different groups of Jews also don't agree about which of them are actually included in the worldwide Jewish community. Ashkenazi (northern European) Jews and those of the Sephardi (Iberian) and Mizrachi (North African and Asian) Jewish communities are discovering that many Africans (in Ethiopia and other countries such as Ghana, Nigeria, South

Africa, and Zimbabwe) and African Americans who call themselves Israelites have been practicing a version of Judaism for centuries, but many in the other Jewish communities don't recognize them as Jews. Of course, those Jews of African descent are not altogether sure that their Ashkenazi cousins should be counted either. Messianic Jews (who practice Judaism but also believe that Jesus is the messiah) don't fit comfortably with those Jews for whom Jesus was just another Jew—possibly a prophet, but definitely not the still-awaited messiah. Hasidic, Ultra-Orthodox (Haredi), and Modern Orthodox Jews don't accept conversions done by any of the liberal Jewish denominations, and Orthodox and Conservative Jews don't accept the Reform, Renewal, Reconstructionist, and Humanist notion that being born of one Jewish parent, mother or father, and being raised as a Jew by that parent are enough to make someone count as Jewish.

Finally, the majority of Jews (in the United States and Israel, the two largest Jewish communities in the world, in that order) aren't part of any religious denomination at all, and for them Judaism is not a religious practice but a kinship network they belong to, often with pride. They consider themselves Jews of the secular or ethnic variety, based on their identification with Jewish culture and heritage (but not religion), and may claim to be Jewish without the stamp of approval of any religious authority. And many Jews, even ones who consider themselves religious, don't necessarily believe in an all-wise and all-knowing God. In fact, the Reconstructionist and Humanist movements were started by people who questioned the existence of such a God. And, of course, there are a number of people who are Jewish by birth but don't identify themselves as Jewish at all. They may convert to other religions, change their names, alter their noses, or simply pretend they have no connection whatsoever, although they may sneak an occasional bagel or have a penchant for saying "*oy*" surprisingly often.

But whose Torah is it, anyway?

Hasidic, Ultra-Orthodox, and Modern Orthodox, Conservative, Reform, Reconstructionist, Renewal, Humanist, Secular, Cultural, Ashkenazi, Israelite, Messianic, Sephardi: all have different ways of being Jewish and different definitions of who is a Jew. So who has the right to say to whom the Torah belongs? The answer has to be all of the above. Jews all along this spectrum can claim an authentic connection to the history, texts, and traditions of what has come to be known as Judaism, and each has a legitimate right to call him- or herself part of the Jewish people, even if he or she doesn't agree with one another's definitions or criteria. All find within Judaism as they understand it the answer to the question of how to live a good life.

The Jews whose Judaism is central to this book aren't a separate group, but can be found among all of the groups delineated above. We are the Jews for whom the answer to living a good, Jewish life is found in the simple biblical exhortation "Justice, justice, you shall pursue" (in Hebrew, "*tzedek, tzedek tirdof*") from the Book of Deuteronomy, chapter 16, verse 20. I would like to think that everyone who identifies as a Jew sees this verse as an important aspect of Jewish ethical teaching. And I also know that not every Jew makes this idea the central tenet of his or her Judaism, but then again, there are many of us who do. In order to fully understand this quotation and those to whom it is the very basis of their Jewish lives, we need to look at (you guessed it) several ways in which we approach the Torah, the first five books of the Hebrew Bible—the text from which this quotation arises and which forms the foundation of the Jewish heritage.

Relating to the Torah is of course not without difficulties. Highlighting the pursuit of justice as a core approach to being Jewish does not shield us from having to deal with the more difficult passages and perspectives we find in the Bible, and in all our ancient texts, that often sit side by side with powerful demands such as the pursuit of justice. Although Richard Dawkins' depiction of the God of the Hebrew Bible in *The God Delusion* as "an appalling role-model, sanctioning gang-rape and genocide" is one-sided and mean-spirited, it wounds because there's more than a kernel of truth to it.[1] We ignore the complexity and downright evils of our tradition at our peril because that leaves us vulnerable to critiques such as those Dawkins levels. Those of us whose Judaism begins with a loving, compassionate God who wants justice for the Jewish people and the world need to reckon with the difficult parts of our tradition if we want to make any sort of reasonable claim about the value of our tradition.

We may find ourselves uneasy today with the Torah. Its injunction of "an eye for an eye" may have been an improvement over systems that permitted revenge on a much larger scale, but the rabbis in the Talmud later decided that the phrase really meant monetary compensation and was not to be taken literally. It's not easy to accept the enmity between Jews and Arabs that is reflected in the biblical story of the exile of Hagar and her son Ishmael. Although it is highly unlikely that the Israelites actually conquered the land of Canaan, the warrior God who commanded the slaughter of the indigenous nations may still disturb our sensibilities, and we must wonder why our ancestors chose to portray God as a conquering hero, even if we rationalize that he was the imagined savior of a people who lived subjugated to the rule of the powerful kingdoms of Egypt and Assyria. We will bristle at rabbinic and medieval discussions about the monetary value of a virgin, or their unflattering remarks about women's virtues or intelligence, even if we find verses that also indicate a more positive view. It just may not be possible to completely ameliorate the negative attitudes or fantasies of revenge harbored by our ancestors, even if we find ways to rationalize them.

Rather, we must begin by acknowledging that some of the texts we inherit are terrible, and we need to give ourselves permission to say so. Perhaps the best way to deal with the difficult texts is by staring them in the face and then using the act of denouncing them as an impetus to change. It is a powerful weapon to name a text as oppressive and to defy it publicly and dramatically. The protests of *agunot*—women who can't remarry because their husbands refuse to divorce them—remind us that some parts of Jewish law are not only wrong but endanger the lives and well-being of women and children. Transgender activists who are angered by the injunction against wearing the clothes of the opposite sex also make this point. The movements for gender and sexual equality and disability rights in Judaism protest those ancient laws and stories that make women, people with disabilities, and sexual minorities into second-class citizens. Of course, contextualizing these texts and spinning out alternative meanings render them less harmful and are also valuable tools for making change, and we need to employ those strategies as well. But sometimes the political act of pointing out and rejecting the evils we find in our tradition can be empowering and positive gestures that leave more room to develop connections to the parts of tradition that are life-giving and that compel us to continue to be in conversation with the Jewish past. And ultimately, if we want to be part of the Jewish people, we must turn away from our anger and look for the sources of our tradition that nurture and support our passion for justice.

When we approach "*tzedek, tzedek tirdof*," this text from the Torah that inspires just that urge in us, it's important that we do so from a variety of approaches. Even though Jews may agree that this text is important, we will connect to it in very different ways, and it will yield many interpretations. Perhaps it's best to begin by putting it in historical context. What is this exhortation doing in the book of Deuteronomy? And what is the book of Deuteronomy anyway?

THE SCHOLARLY APPROACH: HISTORICAL AND LINGUISTIC

When we approach biblical texts historically, we are usually searching for what the text meant in its own time. We are seeking to figure out what we can really know about the lives of our ancestors, if anything. We may learn this based on what scholars who study the Bible have gleaned from textual or archaeological evidence from surrounding cultures. Biblical scholars believe that the Hebrew Bible is a collection of texts written over a period of more than a thousand years before the time of Jesus (or, in Jewish parlance, B.C.E.—before the common era) by multiple authors and skillful editors (often called redactors), with various perspectives from the theological to the liturgical and the literary to the political. The Talmud contains similar complex material that covers, more or less, the next five hundred years of Jewish history.

Historically, the verse "*tzedek, tzedek tirdof* " is set in the context of other laws that describe an ideal legislative system. Biblical scholars agree that the book of Deuteronomy is a recapitulation and elaboration of the laws set out in the other books of Torah (hence its name, which means "second telling of the law"). We know it was written in the form of Moses' farewell speech. It was definitely the "Torah scroll" described in the biblical book called Second Kings. It may have been written in the context of the prophetic era of King Josiah's reign (622 B.C.E.), or it may be based on earlier materials that reflect the times of Moses, even if he wasn't the author. The section in which our verse is found tells us a lot about its meaning. The broad description of civil law emphasizes a utopian vision of a legal system as a moral enterprise. Its primary goal is the creation of a just society through the protection of individuals, and particularly the most vulnerable.

Another scholarly approach examines the language of

the text and the three words themselves. Let us turn first to the word *tzedek*. The term is often translated as "righteousness." Its alternative version, *tzedakah*, came to mean the human obligation to give away some portion of one's wealth or possessions to worthy causes as fundamental to creating a just society. *Tzedek* is justice broadly construed, not as specific laws (for this there are two other terms, *din* and *mishpat*) but as the foundational principle of an ethical society. The repetition of *tzedek* is a literary device that serves to make a word emphatic, as we might do in English with the adjective *very* or *really*. On this basis, we can translate *tzedek, tzedek* as "perfect/honest/true/real/certain justice." The author or editor meant the reader (or listener) to notice: this is an important concept, folks. Using the verb *tirdof*, for which the English "pursue" is a good translation, strengthens this emphasis even more—don't just do it, pursue it!

TRADITIONAL METHODS:
HALAKHAH AND *AGGADAH*

Using the work of scholars is one way to look at the Torah, but Jewish tradition has its own strategies: *halakhah* (roughly, "law") and *aggadah* (roughly, "story").

Halakhah is most often translated as "Jewish law," but those who consider themselves halakhic Jews will tell you that the root of the term *halakhah* is not law. Rather, it comes from the verb "to go." Following *halakhah* means setting out on a path that provides a guide for every aspect of life. It begins with law, the collection of 613 commandments found in the Torah given by God to Moses on Mount Sinai and therefore binding and irrevocable. Interestingly enough, *"tzedek, tzedek tirdof"* is not one of the 613. Its universal, utopian, and generic nature may make it compelling as credo but rather useless as *halakhah*, which is built on detail. From the legal perspective, it doesn't tell us much.

Those who take a halakhic approach would agree that even the 613 laws and commandments that God gave can't be taken only as specific injunctions but, like the other teachings in the Torah, are open to human interpretation and debate about what they mean and how to practice them. While for the most part ancient legal texts (Mishnah, Talmud, and the code of laws called the *Shulhan Arukh*) define the limits of the interpretations, there is a lot of room to maneuver here. A saying from the Mishnah, "Turn it and turn it, for everything is in it," would sum up this approach. The Talmud's recording of both majority and minority opinions, following the interpretations of commentators such as the renowned medieval rabbi called Rashi, and basing opinions on case law in the form of questions and answers (*shelot v'tshuvot*) keep this legal tradition lively. And the resulting legislation is sometimes unpredictable. Still, those who strictly follow Jewish law aren't comfortable making radical and dramatic changes. In these times they rely on a small group of rabbis they consider legal experts to interpret the texts for contemporary circumstances. However, today's leaders tend to be reticent about making sweeping pronouncements, especially concerning laws that have a biblical origin. Those who are more open sometimes find themselves needing to stretch their interpretations, occasionally beyond credulity, in order to preserve their commitment to the letter as well as the spirit of *halakhah* while also accommodating new perspectives and realities in the contemporary world.

Luckily, a strict legal path is not the only interpretive strategy used by rabbinic Judaism. When we are searching for wisdom and guidance about how to apply lessons from the ancient texts to our daily lives, we are compelled to engage in hermeneutics (interpretation). In the Jewish world this hermeneutical tradition is called *aggadah*, and it is a traditional method used to approach Jewish texts alongside *halakhah*. *Midrash* (the method of interpretation) is so central to Jewish thought that we even find it in the biblical text itself. Some aggadic interpreters have suggested that the whole book of Deuteronomy is really one long *midrash* that recapitulates Exodus, Leviticus, and Numbers because it recasts those books into a program for society and emphasizes certain key ideas, one of which is *tzedek*, as we have already seen.

Jewish writers use *midrash* when they have a question about what the Torah leaves out of its story. What was Sarah thinking when Abraham decided to take Isaac to be sacrificed? Why did Moses hit that rock? The rabbis also used *midrash* to explain things that appear to us to be contradictory, such as why there are two creation stories. *Midrash* furthermore explains away things we find rather reprehensible, such as suggesting that the angels were weeping, not cheering, when the Egyptian army was drowned in the sea as they pursued the Israelites during their exodus from Egypt. From the perspective of *midrash*, our tradition encompasses not only laws God commanded but also stories and lessons that are an integral part of a Jewish heritage.

The rabbis of the Talmud found a combination of *halakhah* and *midrash* to be the perfect vehicle to explicate our verse. The main question the Talmud asks about our text is why *tzedek* is repeated. Though biblical scholars provided a simple linguistic answer—it makes the verse emphatic—the ancient rabbis firmly believed that each word of the Torah had its own unique meaning. If the word *tzedek* is repeated, it could only be because the text was talking about two versions of justice, perhaps the origin of the notion that two Jews have (at least) two opinions.

Giving meanings to the two kinds of *tzedek* has kept Jewish interpreters quite busy over the centuries. One example of this strategy reveals a lot. In the Talmud (Sanhedrin 32b), we learn that the first *tzedek* teaches that we must pursue strict justice, while the second *tzedek* means we must engage in compromise, a strategy that surely will come in handy when facing all those opinions. The meaning of strict justice is not discussed in this passage because it is carefully laid out in Deuteronomy and later commentaries.

To illustrate what is meant by compromise, the Talmud gives us two practical examples, in keeping with the notion that justice is derived not only in courts but in our everyday lives. The first is a simple case. Two boats meet on a river, so one must give way to the other, or they will both sink. One yields to the other, resulting in positive consequences for both. But things aren't so simple in the case of two camels who meet going up a narrow mountain path. One must go first, so how to decide who yields? The rabbis provide a few solutions. If one camel is carrying a heavier burden, that one goes first. If one camel approached first, then that one goes first. But if all factors are equal, they must agree to a compromise, and the one that ends up going first must compensate the other for the privilege. One of the values of this passage for our purposes is to remind us that holding lofty principles and achieving justice often require sweating the small stuff: compromise, negotiation, and a scrupulous attention to detail. And it comes in handy when we're dealing with real-life situations where disagreements frequently arise.

The Kotzker Rebbe, another nineteenth-century Hasidic teacher, parses the doubling of *tzedek* in another way, to suggest that the first *tzedek* reflects the means we use to pursue justice, while the second relates to the actual ends, the *tzedek* we wish to accomplish. Just as the rabbis suggested, we must use just tactics to achieve our goals. In other words, to *do* justice requires that we also *be* just.

MAKING IT PERSONAL

Which gets us back to our original proposition that there are many ways to express and experience being Jewish. But knowing about the wonderful values in Jewish tradition won't mean much unless we apply these ideas to our own lives. To take this to a personal level means that we subscribe to the proposition that we can define Judaism not only by the legacy handed down to us by past generations but also by what we as

Jews create today. We can't forget what we have inherited, and to be part of the Jewish story is, by definition, to build on what we find usable or malleable from our past. But it's not only the connection to the past that keeps Judaism alive; without the whole assortment of Jewish groups and individuals and the things they do now, Judaism could not survive as a living entity. To be a Jew means to make the claim that what we do is Jewish even if other Jews may not appreciate our interpretations and may even question our authenticity or challenge our right to speak in a Jewish voice. History may decide that our claim (or theirs) is not valid, but it's unlikely given the model of multiple opinions for multiple Jews. And even so, that shouldn't deter us. If we want the answer to the question "Who does the Torah belong to?" to be "It belongs to us," then we must make our lives the text—and live so that we see our words and deeds not simply repeating but also adding something to the Jewish story. We are obligated to demand our own version of strict justice, and sometimes to work toward compromise when necessary.

Two examples may illustrate for us how to take these particular teachings of our tradition and bring them to life. One is from Arik Aschermann, the leader of Rabbis for Human Rights in Israel, and the other is suggested by Jonathan Kremer, a graphic designer and Hebrew calligrapher in Philadelphia.

Aschermann asks why *tzedek* is repeated in our verse, and suggests, very concretely, that one stands for the Palestinian right to their land, and the second to their right to participate in nonviolent protest when their land is being taken away. His commentary was written to encourage his fellow Israelis to join a Palestinian demonstration in the town of Bilin in 2005 where, in defiance of the decree of the Israeli High Court, the government persisted in building the barrier wall between Israel and Palestine in a way that caused irreversible damage and the uprooting of fruit trees. In addition, the army decided to crack down on nonviolent protests.[2]

Kremer concludes that justice has two dimensions: one to support justice for Jews and the other to work for justice for others in society. His specific reference is to the pride those in his town of Lower Merion feel because Jewish residents take care to educate their children in the local public schools, which they support with their tax dollars. Kremer's second specific *tzedek* is to encourage Jewish residents of Lower Merion to fight for better public education in the neighboring city of Philadelphia, where students don't have textbooks or working water fountains, let alone small classes or instruction in foreign language, art, or music, or access to other advanced or specialized courses that are available to Lower Merion's children.[3]

In this book we will examine other examples of how Jews have used tradition to seek justice in the areas of race, sexuality, gender, poverty, the environment, and the pursuit of peace. Those of us whose Judaism is grounded in pursuing justice make good use of all the methods I suggest here for living with what we inherit as Jews, for better or worse, as well as for shaping a Jewish future. We know and use Jewish sources, whether we understand them as law, history, story, or all of the above. We discern which Jewish texts inspire our vision, what context they come from, how to interpret them, and what to do with the ones that make us uncomfortable or even angry. And we act in ways that allow us to feel not only connected to a Jewish past but also like we are creating a Jewish future by the way we live and work in the present.

1

Sexuality

Judaism can be relied on for healthy attitudes toward sex. Those of us who pursue justice find rich resources for a liberating sexual ethic, though this may not be immediately obvious, given the many more than two opinions on sexuality we find among Jews.

Jewish views, as you can imagine, are rather complicated. The ancient rabbis recognized that women have sexual needs, but weren't always so happy about the fact. God is male, yet has no sex. Tradition saw men's sexuality as a source of power but thought it also needed careful supervision. Celibacy is not part of Jewish tradition, but some have followed ascetic practices. Views of birth control depend on the era and how urgently Jews perceive the need to increase the Jewish population. Abortion is neither murder nor simply a matter of choice. Homosexuality is rarely mentioned until the contemporary period, when it has been treated respectfully, even in some (but not all) Orthodox circles. Commonly accepted behaviors that are strictly prohibited in the Bible, such as masturbation, are widely accepted today, and sexual experimentation between unmarried partners is even encouraged. It is no wonder that outsiders are often confused

by Jewish views of sexuality. They just don't conform to contemporary secular or Christian norms.

American consumer culture has its own contradictions.
It sells sex while conservative social forces seek to limit sexual
freedom outside of marriage and procreative freedom within
it. Sexuality and reproduction, once inextricably linked, now
can be considered independently of each other because of
contraception and other medical advances. At the same time,
the current threat of new sexually transmitted diseases has
had a profound effect on the sexual attitudes and behaviors
of young people, making them much more cautious and fearful of sex than my generation was. The lesbian, gay, bisexual,
and transgender (LGBT) movement has created new under-
standings of same-sex erotic attractions and gendered lives,
and the feminist movement has brought women's perspectives on sexuality into public conversations. Jews are not exempt from having to think through and adjust to these
sweeping changes and contradictory impulses in our culture, too.

Maybe the best place to start is the Song of Songs, a series of passionate poems of love and desire between young
lovers. These poems were collected and became (a controversial) book of the Hebrew Bible; a midrashic reinterpreta-
tion turned the text into the passionate love story between
God and Israel, which made it acceptable to tradition as a religious book. But the Bible preserves the sexually bold form
of its writing, and sections are read aloud in synagogues on
the Sabbath during the holiday of Passover. In the Song of
Songs, we find lyrics of desire and seduction, such as these:

The roundings of thy thighs are like the links of a chain,
The work of the hands of a skilled workman.
Thy navel is like a round goblet,
Wherein no mingled wine is wanting;
Thy belly is like a heap of wheat
Set about with lilies.
Thy two breasts are like two fawns
That are twins of a gazelle. (7:2b–4)

The speakers and subjects in the songs are both men and
women (although it's lovely to imagine a God who thought of
his people in this way), and this book provides strong evidence for sexual equality between men and women in the literary life of ancient Israel. Not surprisingly, it is read today by
gay and lesbian couples, too, since the speaker never reveals
his or her identity. Also the text celebrates the joy of sex but
doesn't tie it either to procreation or to marriage.

Until the past few decades, sex and procreation were in-
separable. Today, the use of birth control is widespread,
pregnancy can be terminated safely through abortion, and
conception may take place in the laboratory and the hospital
as well as the bedroom. These developments call into question the simple connection between sex and procreation.
The Talmud makes procreation a paramount value (the first
commandment in the Bible is, after all, "be fruitful and multiply") and accepts sexual pleasure as a positive corollary of
the only activity through which that could have taken place.
But Jewish legal tradition also did not make just a simple connection between sex and procreation. *Halakhah* permits all

sexual activity for married heterosexual couples, including oral and anal sex. Sexual pleasure within marriage is encouraged even in cases where procreation is not possible, such as infertility and old age. Jewish law even includes a marital obligation called *onah*, requiring a man to provide sexual pleasure for his wife, although the woman's obligation is never mentioned.

During the Middle Ages sexuality became even more highly valued as a part of Jewish religious life. In medieval mystical tradition, kabbalists reinterpreted the heterosexual sex act as a mirror of divine connection between male and female emanations of God. To celebrate heterosexual sex as a reflection of the divine gave it special status. They saw the Sabbath as a particularly appropriate time for sexual relations between husband and wife, channeling sexual activity into religious fervor.

In a well-known medieval hymn, "L'cha Dodi," which is sung weekly in the Friday evening liturgy, the Sabbath is imagined as queen, bride, and beloved, revealing the connection of the sexual and spiritual. Taking kabbalistic ideas about sexuality as a mirror of the divine realm to a logical conclusion, messianic movements of Sabbati Zvi and Jacob Frank used sexual imagery and language in the seventeenth and eighteenth centuries as part of their efforts to bring about a more perfect world.

While medieval rabbis emphasized sexual pleasure in marriage, images of woman as seductress abounded. The legend of Lilith is a prime example. She was invented to explain why the Bible has two creation stories. In the first, male and female are created together; in the second, the female is created from the "rib" or side of the sleeping male. One ancient *midrash* suggested that the stories were actually about two different women. Eve was the second wife, created from Adam's rib; Lilith was the first, created along with Adam and then exiled. According to medieval legend, she was banished because she demanded equality in her relationship with Adam and especially because she wanted to be on top during sex. In past eras, women tied a red ribbon on cribs to scare away Lilith, who was thought to come around and kill babies in revenge for being sent away. Today, Lilith is one of the celebrated heroes of the Jewish feminist movement.

Despite its image of ultra-piety today, Hasidism joined sexuality and spirituality to challenge the very strict traditionalism of its time and place. As a revivalist movement that began in Poland in the seventeenth century, Hasidism followed the medieval mystical and messianic traditions and made sexual energy a conduit between this world and the world of the divine, incorporating a sexual dimension into spiritual observance. The swaying movements of men at prayer simulated movement during sexual intercourse, and the intense fervor of their praying and dancing created an erotically charged same-sex environment.

The nineteenth-century shift from arranged marriage to companionate marriage in Europe also affected Jewish life. Yiddish writers, in works such as *The Dybbuk*, *Yentl the Yeshiva Boy*, and the stories that became *Fiddler on the Roof*, depicted marriage based on romantic love and attraction, rather than on the institution of the matchmaker (*shadchan*), who worked with parents to set up marriages. Companionate marriage challenged the authority of the Jewish family and brought back the unbridled romantic energy that was present in the Song of Songs.

Sexuality was a dominant theme in the modern era. Zionism portrayed the "new Hebrew man" as highly masculine and sexualized. At the same time, the writings of Sigmund Freud (to which Jewish intellectuals paid a good deal of attention) contributed to a new openness about the meaning of sexuality and its relationship to human psychological and physical health. He had a very positive impact on making discussions about sex public in the Jewish community.

Liberal feminists, like liberal Jews in general, have rejected the laws of *niddah* that regulate sexual behavior in marriage. However, Orthodox feminists—and there are many—have redefined this practice as a means of sexual liberation. They assert that the time connected to their menstrual cycles, when they are not obligated to have sexual relations with their husbands, provides a form of sexual freedom. The laws give them the power to have some control over when they resume their sexual relations each month, and this control is particularly useful for couples where the sexual relationship may be negative or even abusive. In positive sexual relationships, Orthodox women claim that the period of abstinence increases desire and pleasure by making the sexual connection both holy and special. Other Orthodox feminists suggest that the ritual immersion that marks the end of their period of separation is itself sexually empowering. An Orthodox woman ends *niddah* by going to the *mikveh* (a public ritual bath), where she washes herself completely, removes every extraneous particle from her body (dead skin, hanging cuticles, loose hairs, and so on), and then, completely naked, immerses herself in the ritual bath. This private experience is a prelude to having sexual relations with her husband, which, by law, takes place immediately after the immersion. Some Orthodox women claim that this ritual calls attention to and enhances the sexual experience.

Contemporary liberal Jewish feminists also have exhibited a strong interest in the Jewish mystical tradition, in which God has feminine traits. Some feminists celebrate Shekinah, for example, which is a feminine noun used in the Torah for the shining presence of God. In Jewish mysticism she represents the feminine aspect of the divine. Jewish feminists write and incorporate into worship prayers to Shekinah, which often allude to the medieval idea that the divine union between God and Shekinah mirrors the sexual union between husband and wife. Feminists have also reinstituted the holiday of Rosh Hodesh, the celebration of the new moon. At one point in ancient times, this holiday was designated as a special day for women. Contemporary feminists link Rosh Hodesh to women's menstrual cycle, and use it to connect women's sexual and spiritual dimensions through special women-only observances including song, prayer, and conversation. Through these rituals and interpretations, women can claim a more positive relationship to their bodies and to themselves as sexual beings. Through these new prayers and practices, feminist Jews have emphasized the value of sex as a vehicle for intimacy.

Jewish feminists understand sexuality positively and link it with the spiritual. In this way, we have claimed a place for women's sexuality in Judaism and have emphasized the parts of Jewish tradition in which heterosexual sex is valued and holy. It is not surprising that women who retain a connection to Judaism would want to embrace the parts of tradition that respect women's sexuality rather than the aspects that denigrate it. Through reinterpreting and reclaiming the positive traditions, Jewish women have made an important place for themselves within Jewish life.

After World War II, Jews became comfortable in U.S. society. Anti-Semitism receded. Nonetheless, stereotypes of Jews are still common, and they abound in popular-culture novels, music, and films, and, most prevalently, in humor. They express how other Americans feel about Jews having power and assimilating into American society, but they often take the form of commentary on Jewish sexuality. Unlike the stereotypes of hypersexual Jewish men and women the Nazis produced, sexual stereotypes of Jews in the United States are differentiated by gender. The Jewish man often is seen as effeminate, weak, and unmanly—à la Woody Allen. The Jewish woman is presented as a "Jewish American princess" or JAP (probably an allusion to the derogatory term used for Japanese Americans during World War II and afterward). The princess is sexually passive, consumed only by the desire to shop and to beautify herself through cosmetics, surgery, and diet. While the stereotypes about Jewish men were common throughout modern history, the princess stereotype is peculiar to the American scene.

Study and prayer are highly valued in Judaism, so it is not surprising that Jews are known as the "people of the book." Jewish masculinity is defined as intellectual prowess. In European Jewish societies, women were expected to care for the economic well-being of the family while men studied. A pious family would take in students so that young men could study without worrying about making money, and a "good match" for a young woman was to marry a scholar. Consequently, American standards of masculinity, defined by physical beauty and strength, were not important in traditional Jewish society.

While Zionism challenged the scholarly image, and Israeli men even today do not suffer from the "sissy" stereotype, Jewish men in the United States still do. The stereotype has stuck. Orthodox men who follow the cultural norms of earlier Jewish societies are expected to be scholars, and women are expected both to care for the home and to have an occupation. Although assimilated American men are no longer expected to be students, they tend to follow more cerebral and less physical career paths. The "nebbish" as portrayed by Woody Allen is very interested in sex but, to outward appearances, is weak and unattractive. Jokes about effeminate Jewish men, such as the one in the film *Airplane*, in which someone is given a small two-page pamphlet entitled "Jews and Sports," cause them severe discomfort. Figures such as the baseball player Hank Greenberg and the wrestler Bill Goldberg are Jewish heroes because they reveal the other side of the stereotype and allow Jewish men to take pride in the kind of masculinity respected in U.S. society.

Other jokes about Jewish men's lack of sexual endowment (such as the suggestion that Jewish women are bad at math because they are told that this [finger gesture denoting an inch] is six inches) make for further discomfort. There are Jewish writers who suggest that masculinity can take different cultural forms, and they urge Jewish men to embrace gentleness as virility in order to mitigate this problem.

FORBIDDEN SEXUAL RELATIONSHIPS

The ancient textual tradition forbids many sexual behaviors and relationships that are common and acceptable in today's society while allowing some now forbidden. Although ancient Jews practiced polygamy and prostitution and accepted sexual encounters between unmarried men and women and oral and anal sex within marriage, they prohibited many other sexual practices that are commonly accepted today, such as masturbation, homosexual relations, sex before (and outside of) marriage, romantic love, and sexual relationships with non-Jews. These matters require Jews to rethink them. If we are interested in justice, then we need to support those whose sexuality is not considered "normal" by society's standards.

In most Orthodox and Hasidic communities, arranged marriages are the norm, and young people who join these communities welcome them. In some instances, women join in order remove themselves from pressure to be sexual before marriage. More liberal Orthodox communities, on the other hand, have come to terms with sex before marriage, and the "*tefillin* date" is a common experience. Traditionally, young men must say morning prayers wearing a ritual object wrapped around their head and left arm known as *tefillin*. If they stay overnight with their dates, they need to be prepared to pray in the morning. The decision to carry *tefillin* along on a date acknowledges this possibility.

Liberal Judaism has come to terms more readily with the expansion of acceptable sexual relationships. Although remaining committed to marriage as the best option, liberal Jews have abandoned other prohibitions around sexuality. Divorce was always an acceptable practice in Jewish law, so it was not difficult to accept serial monogamy as a norm. Single adults having sex is considered appropriate and even desirable for their mental health. Masturbation is assumed to be a normal part of sexual experimentation. Teens are taught about and encouraged to participate in safe sexual activities, provided they treat the partners they choose with respect. The laws of family purity are no longer practiced, and so menstrual rules of intermittent abstinence do not govern sex within marriage. Gays and lesbians also are respected, and liberal Judaism has begun to tackle issues related to bisexual and transgender Jews. While all of these issues have required much thought and some anguish, dealing with the issue of gay rights has thus far been the greatest challenge to Jewish liberals and traditionalists alike, although, ironically, prohibitions against homosexuality are less severe than those against other sexual practices.

Homosexuality is mentioned only rarely in the canonical texts of Jewish tradition. The Hebrew Bible does not mention female same-sex relationships at all, although later commentaries suggest that the reference in Leviticus to forbidden "practices of Egypt" is about female-female marriage. Leviticus forbids male same-sex acts and describes them as *toevah*, an "abomination" (although the Hebrew word is difficult to translate, this is how most English versions render it). This prohibition occurs twice, and the second time it carries the penalty of death, although even contemporary Orthodox leaders reject the death penalty for this infraction. Recently, scholars have debated the meaning of this interdiction, although it received scant attention prior to the advent of gay liberation. Clearly, the prohibition does not refer to gay relationships as they exist today since such relationships were unknown in ancient times. It is more likely a reference to a particular sexual act—probably anal intercourse—that was prohibited along with other practices either to distinguish Israelite practices from those of their neighbors or to indicate an abhorrence of mixing together things that were perceived not to belong together—in this case, bodily fluids; in others, fabrics, animals, or foods. In any case, it was one prohibition among many concerning sexual behaviors, and was not singled out as it is today.

The story of Sodom in the book of Genesis, which describes a group of men who demand homosexual sex from guests and strangers to the town, is the only other instance where a male homosexual act is mentioned in the Hebrew Bible. While Christian commentators take this event as a condemnation of homosexuality (hence the term *sodomite*), Jewish tradition is more concerned about how rude and inhospitable such a request would be in the case of either gender. Contemporary commentators have seen love between men in the biblical friendship of David and Jonathan, and love between women in Ruth and Naomi's relationship. No evidence exists to indicate that the authors of the stories intended such readings of the texts. However, the relationships are described in the biblical text in a way that leaves open the possibility of midrashic interpretations and elaborations that would allow gay men and lesbians to imagine that they might have had biblical progenitors.

Following biblical law, the Talmud prohibits two men from sleeping under the same blanket. However, a minority opinion permits this, expressing the idea that Jewish men would not engage in homosexual acts, even if given the opportunity. The Talmud permits women known to engage in female homoerotic acts to marry priests (who could only marry virgins), because these acts are not considered sex, which requires penile penetration. It also assumes that these women, despite having relations with other women, are going to marry men, as would likely have been the case in ancient times with arranged marriages. Similarly, medieval commentaries instruct husbands to punish their wives if they discover them to be engaging in homoerotic acts with other women, but this is considered a minor matter, not a cause for concern. The medieval period also produced male homoerotic poetry, but we do not know the extent to which this indicates widespread behavior or simply an interest in copying Arabic poetic conventions of the times. Together these written sources tell us that homosexual behavior was clearly known in Jewish societies throughout ancient times, but it was not considered a disruption to the social fabric. It was also not a justice concern.

In the modern period there are literary sources that mention homosexual relationships. Yiddish literature has a recurring theme of cross-dressing women who are thought to carry men's souls in women's bodies. But until the gay liberation movement, homosexuality was rarely discussed publicly in the Jewish world, and there was a commonly held notion, not unlike that expressed in the Talmud, that Jews simply were not susceptible to same-sex attractions. This idea was shattered in the 1970s and 1980s. Many Jews began to identify themselves publicly as gay and lesbian, and the community had to face the reality of openly gay and lesbian people who wanted to join synagogues, raise children, and serve as teachers and rabbis.

The early reactions were primarily disbelief, resulting in the invisibility of gay and lesbian concerns for quite some time. In the 1970s, gay Jews developed new synagogues in New York, San Francisco, and Los Angeles, and they were actually welcomed by a few Jewish organizations in their early years, although most ignored them. The liberal Jewish community received *Nice Jewish Girls*, an anthology of coming-out stories of Jewish lesbians, with curiosity, while Orthodox leaders placed its editor and authors under a ban.[1]

Gay men and lesbians demanded and began to find acceptance in the liberal Jewish community by the late 1980s. Gay synagogues applied to affiliate with religious movements, and rabbinical schools were challenged to ordain openly lesbian and gay clergy. A number of authors published books and articles demanding the attention of the organized Jewish community. Most recently, many rabbis have begun to perform same-sex marriages at the request of Jewish couples. Although Orthodox leaders are still unwilling to accept people who identify themselves publicly as gay or lesbian, growing numbers of Jews who do are challenging their positions. Given that there are no legal barriers to the acceptance of lesbian sex and only minimal barriers to gay male sex (some have argued that abstinence from anal sex should be the only criterion for Orthodox acceptance of gay men), it is quite possible that this situation will change over time.

The liberal Jewish community has been remarkably supportive and welcoming of gay men and lesbians who seek to be involved. Many rabbis perform commitment ceremonies, and many synagogues welcome gay and lesbian couples, provide a caring educational environment for their children, support families who are dealing with daughters and sons coming out, and allow gay men and lesbians to serve in leadership positions. Gay men and lesbians, in turn, accept the ideals of the Jewish community. They understand that being welcomed is predicated on a model of monogamous marriage, child rearing, and the nuclear family. (Of course, the same strictures apply to heterosexuals.) Other sexual life choices simply are not as welcome.

Bisexuality is another matter. The main factor in many Jews' acceptance of gay men and lesbians is an understanding of same-sex attraction and behavior as not chosen, and therefore not amenable to change. As such, it must be accepted as a variation that is part of God's plan for human nature. But there is still discomfort with the idea that people are choosing lives that do not conform to the heterosexual ideal. According to most official Jewish religious groups' pronouncements, if choice is involved, the individual should choose the path that conforms to the majority's standards—that is, heterosexuality. Bisexuals claim that they are sexually attracted to both men and women and that gender is not a significant factor in selecting a sexual partner. This idea challenges fundamental assumptions about sexual choices in ways that strictly gay and lesbian sexuality does not.

Jewish communities are only beginning to support transgender rights. The first transgender rabbi was ordained by the Reform movement at the dawn of the twenty-first century. Transgender Jews are using text and *midrash* to tell their stories and make their demands for acceptance in the Jewish community in vivid and creative ways. They also raise questions that challenge rigid assumptions about the existence of only two genders in Jewish communal settings. Transgender people experience Judaism differently when they transition, and that experience makes us ever more aware of how gender differences are expressed in Jewish settings. The simple acts of not making assumptions about someone's gender, providing unisex bathrooms in public Jewish spaces, and making sure we know what pronoun transgendered people prefer to be used in reference to them make a big difference.

The State of Israel has been surprisingly open to the inclusion of gay men and lesbians as well. Although the Orthodox have complete authority in matters of marriage and other issues of personal status and have made gay pride parades occasions for screaming battles and threats of violence as well as celebrations, Israel is ultimately a secular state and has proven welcoming to gay men and lesbians. They serve openly in the army, are entitled to domestic partnership benefits in some cases, and in recent years have developed a gay and lesbian subculture similar to that in the United States, including publications, media exposure, social and political groups, and public meeting places. As most non-Orthodox Jews in Israel are not religious, the question of gay rabbis, marriages, and synagogues is not as important there. Gay synagogues do flourish around the world, however, and the World Congress of Lesbian, Gay, Bisexual, and Transgender Jewish Organizations has representation in Latin America, Canada, Western Europe, and Australia.

MARRIAGE EQUALITY

No issue lends itself to Jewish concerns for justice better than marriage equality. Marriage in the United States is framed as a religious issue, even though secular courts and legislatures adjudicate it, so Jewish support is important to success in that legal battle in many key states. From a Jewish perspective, supporting marriage equality involves three crucial aspects: economic justice, public and communal recognition of love, and the protection of children.

Marriage in Judaism has an economic basis. The text of

the ancient Jewish marriage contract, the *ketubah*, was an exchange of property: a man would "give" his daughter in marriage to another man. Her sexual status determined her economic value (virgins were worth more than widows; virginity had to be proven through physical evidence or the contractual terms were open to renegotiation). The husband was contractually obligated to provide the basic necessities of life for his wife, who was then his property. While a notion of women as property is offensive to modern sensibilities, the Jewish marriage contract provided economic protection for women at a time when their choices were limited. Jewish marriage contracts are clearly designed to establish economic well-being for the parties involved. The fact that the contract provided conjugal rights (*onah*) for the wife is considered by many to be an important dimension of the transaction. *Onah* indicates an understanding of women as sexual beings and recognizes their humanity. It eventually led the way for a change in understanding gender relationships in marriage.

The political and economic emancipation of women over the past few centuries has changed the economics of marriage and the marriage contract. While traditional Jews still use the ancient contract, and some liberal Jews also retain it for symbolic reasons, most contemporary contracts for liberal Jews have been recast to omit economic factors. This change is based on the assumption that women no longer need these ancient protections. In addition, the text of the traditional *ketubah*, as it has been preserved, no longer reflects contemporary sensibilities of gender equality. What remains, however, is the consciousness that marriage had economic consequences for Jews under Jewish law. It still does for some—the traditional *ketubah* is the only contract valid in Orthodox communities, where the economic consequences of Jewish marriage and divorce are still a serious concern for women.

In contrast, civil marriage affects the well-being, economic and emotional, of gay and lesbian couples. The lack of benefits has caused severe financial and emotional hardship for gay and lesbian couples. Married couples automatically share property and inherit from one another, are defined as next of kin in medical decision making, are allowed to adopt each other's children, receive each other's pension and health benefits, file joint tax returns, and provide citizenship for immigrant spouses. While marriage (or civil unions) at the state level guarantees some of these rights, the vast array of federal benefits remains unavailable. Hence, for many Jewish gay men and lesbians, the reason to fight for same-sex marriage is based, in part, on the principle of economic justice as reflected in the traditional Jewish recognition of the economic basis of marriage.

PUBLIC COMMITMENT

Marriage also has other purposes in Judaism. Marriage is about sanctifying a loving relationship. It is an opportunity to give public, communal support to a committed partnership between two individuals. It is a chance to express faith in the relationship through the acknowledgment of the community that supports it. Marriage celebrates the religious values of long-term commitment, faithfulness, and the willingness to share life's joys and sorrows. The nature of the commitment no longer is about a woman's protection by and subservience to a man but has been "reconstructed" to emphasize equality between the partners. The committed nature of the relationship is paramount and enforces deeply held religious values.

From a Jewish justice perspective there is no difference between purposes for heterosexual and same-sex marriage, so it is unjust to deprive gay and lesbian couples of this opportunity. The partners pledge the same commitment to love and devotion in the presence of a loving community. And there is no evidence to show that the intent to make a lasting commitment is different in either case. Same-sex couples seek to be married within the Jewish tradition for the same reasons that heterosexual couples do: they see this public declaration of their commitment in religious terms. Same-sex couples know that the state does not at this time validate their marriages, but they want to be considered married in the eyes of God and the Jewish people. They seek to invest the ceremony with religious meaning. The principle of religious equality requires that these expressions of love be given the same societal validation, regardless of the genders of the partners involved.

Liberal Judaism rejects differences based on gender in the wedding ceremony. Equal partners exchange rings and vows; both parties sign the marriage contract, and they are often pronounced "life partners" rather than the antiquated "husband and wife." Often, both parties break a glass at the conclusion of the wedding, a role traditionally assigned only to the groom. This egalitarian approach defines a marriage ceremony as an interdependent transaction between equals and removes any assumption that those equals must have different genders.

PRO-NATALISM

The other main purpose of Jewish marriage is to control and encourage procreation. In today's society, procreation outside of marriage is not stigmatized as greatly as it once was, although single parents are often not granted social status equivalent to that of a married couple. Married people without children are also more common, and childlessness within marriage is more acceptable, but Jewish values are strongly pro-natalist. The shrinking of the Jewish community through the Nazi genocide, on one hand, and factors related to assimilation, on the other, produce a strong communal value in support of having and raising children. The Jewish population has remained stable over the past few decades, but Jews form a very small percentage of the world population. The threat of extinction makes Jewish leaders passionately committed to population growth, even in the face of larger societal concerns about the need for global population control.

While many people assume that same-sex marriages are childless, this is far from the truth. Media images of the gay family are replacing stereotypic notions of gay antipathy to children. The availability of children for adoption to single parents (and even to gay couples), the growing awareness and acceptance of alternative insemination methods, and the presence of children from previous heterosexual unions make children commonplace in gay and lesbian communities. In the Jewish community in particular, one can speak of a gay and lesbian baby boom. Gay and lesbian Jews are often attracted to involvement in the Jewish community. They want children and a place for those children to develop Jewish identities and connections. And this desire is often connected to a wish to marry, for legal protection for children if for no other reason.

What, then, is the unique contribution of Jewish groups to this quest for marriage equality? They have pioneered the development and legitimization of ceremonies of commitment for same-sex couples, and those ceremonies in turn form the basis for advocating civil marriage. They manifest this support through public advocacy and political activities on behalf of the legalization of same-sex marriage in the United States and Canada.

The first Reconstructionist Rabbinical Association's *Rabbi's Manual*, published in 1997, provided a ceremony to celebrate same-sex relationships. Rabbi's manuals generally provide guidance about how to conduct ceremonies for life cycle events from weddings to housewarmings. The presence of this ceremony in the manual made Reconstructionist support of gay and lesbian weddings official. It signified that performing such ceremonies was indeed legitimate and in keeping with the Reconstructionist movement's policies, not simply a matter of personal preference or individual conscience. The introduction to the ceremony indicates it is in response to

> a great need to create formulas and procedures whereby this generally marginalized segment of our community can publicly legitimate, formally validate or otherwise rightfully express principles of love and dedication, and so move into the mainstream.[2]

The ceremony is stunning in its acknowledgment that the love between gay men and lesbians is worthy of religious and communal recognition. The rabbi is encouraged to say:

> For so long in our people's history, the love of two men or two women was not a cause for rejoicing. Today we rejoice—we thank the source of life for giving us life and the capacity to love, for sustaining us in life and for enabling us to reach this joyous moment.[3]

Rabbis and Jewish organizations have also participated in the struggles for civil marriage for same-sex couples in the United States and Canada. All the major non-Orthodox groups are on record supporting civil marriage for same-sex couples. Their resolutions always demand that gay and lesbian couples should not be denied access to the benefits of marriage automatically bestowed on heterosexual couples. They also suggest that religious voices have been misrepresented as uniformly opposed to equality. They furthermore encourage their synagogues to extend benefits to same-sex employees, recommend the giving of *tzedakah* (charitable contributions) to secular same-sex marriage advocacy organizations, and urge rabbis to educate their constituencies about the importance of these issues through sermons, premarital counseling, and newsletter articles. They also encourage rabbis to become involved and speak out in public forums, based on a commitment to religious liberty as well as economic and political justice.

Rabbis have been involved in a variety of efforts to support these resolutions, both in states and provinces that have legalized same-sex marriage and in those areas where same-sex marriage has been denied through passage of defense-of-marriage acts. They have defended marriage equality where the issue is being contested through constitutional amendments to ban gay marriage or initiatives to legalize civil unions or gay marriage. Many rabbis give sermons or write articles for synagogue bulletins and letters to editors of local newspapers and to elected officials. In addition, rabbis in many cities are active with groups such as the Freedom to Marry Coalition, organized by the Lambda Legal Defense and Education Fund; they have worked on interfaith events, organized coalitions, and performed public ceremonies in areas where they are legal and in those where they are illegal.

In addition to legislative initiatives, Jews have pursued strategies using the courts. A 1995 case, *Shahar v. Bowers*, demonstrated how the Jewish acceptance of same-sex marriage could be evoked. Shahar, a public employee in Georgia, claimed that she was fired from her position because she participated in a same-sex marriage ceremony. Her lawyers presented a religious discrimination argument as part of their case. Shahar lost at the federal district level, and the Supreme Court decided not to hear the case on appeal, but the point was made.

Jewish support of marriage equality establishes a warrant for Judaism to define same-sex marriage as a deeply held religious belief. On that basis a Jewish group could claim the right to perform same-sex marriages as a dimension of First Amendment religious liberty. Jews can initiate legal cases on that basis, although most lawyers see that strategy as impractical given the current ideological bias of our justice system.

Of course, there is Jewish opposition to marriage equality, from right and left. The Orthodox oppose gay rights. On the opposite end of the spectrum, a goodly number of Jews can't support this issue because their understanding of separation of church and state applies to keeping secular laws out of gay marriage as well as heterosexual marriage. And many feminist Jews believe that marriage is an institution that has disadvantaged women over the centuries and should be abolished, not broadened to include others.

Still, marriage equality is an issue that many Jews have embraced wholeheartedly as a logical dimension of the Jewish justice agenda. Advocating for gay men and lesbians to participate in religious wedding ceremonies with full civil rights has been an important part of a liberal Jewish program for the past decade. Rabbis and congregations have been in the forefront of challenging the idea that all religious groups oppose marriage equality. Jews are well aware that this issue is far from resolved, in either the Jewish or secular worlds, and that they are in a strategic position to play an important role as the debate over this issue unfolds.

In June 2007, the New York State Assembly, with the support of Governor Eliot Spitzer, passed a same-sex marriage bill similar to the one in Massachusetts. Newspaper articles quoted three Jews: an ecstatic Rabbi Sharon Kleinbaum, leader of New York's LGBT congregation Congregation Beth Simhat Torah, who led the fight; one Orthodox assemblyman from Brooklyn who was in active opposition; and the Speaker of the House, Sheldon Silver, also Orthodox, who was instrumental in bringing the bill out of committee. Silver asserted that he would not impose his religious views on others. Three Jews, two opinions, and one vote for justice.

2

Gender Justice

"Do justly" were the words of the biblical prophet Micah that were carved on the outside wall of the Reform synagogue in Brooklyn that I attended while growing up. I took those words to heart, making them the theme of the speech I gave upon completing religious school in tenth grade. The talk focused on Jewish commitment to the civil rights and anti-poverty movements, issues that were uppermost in my mind in the early 1960s. I had no doubt that if I were to choose a career (not something girls thought that much about in those days, but it was in the back of my mind, to be sure), I would want to be a rabbi. I saw rabbis marching in Selma and speaking out for civil rights. Jews were committed to "doing justly," and I thought that would be a good way to make a contribution.

Gender, on the other hand, was a term I learned in high school French to differentiate masculine and feminine nouns. It had nothing to do with justice. Although there was no language for it then, gender injustice was what I would begin to experience as I seriously contemplated becoming a rabbi. Since I lived in the world of liberal Judaism, it never occurred to me that women could not be rabbis—what in our commitment to "do justly" would preclude it? But when I sent an inquiry about rabbinical training and the postcard came back addressed to "Robert," and then when I attended a seminar where only the boys were invited to a special session on applying to rabbinical school, I got the message loud and clear. I put my dream on hold.

Just a few years later, women in American society were beginning to realize that there were many things they might have wanted to do but weren't allowed or encouraged to do, and a revolution began. Called women's liberation, it opened up many avenues, and being a rabbi turned out to be one of them. Pursuing my earlier dream, I decided to attend the Reconstructionist Rabbinical College. (Hebrew Union had started ordaining women, too. It turns out that institution had actually been admitting them for years. They could study but were denied ordination.) I graduated in 1976, one of the first half dozen women ordained officially as rabbis in Jewish history, although we later discovered there were other women who had served in rabbi-like jobs (and one who was actually ordained in Germany in the 1930s but died in the Holocaust).

Although I switched from Reform to Reconstructionism, I never lost my commitment to a prophetic Judaism that puts the pursuit of justice first. I just added the topic of gender justice to the top of my list. Women rabbis participated in creating a Judaism that made room for women's equality and the celebration of women's differences. I was proud to be involved in the development of what has come to be known as Feminist Judaism.

Feminist Judaism is a rethinking of Judaism from the perspectives of women. The ideas and writings that have been preserved and validated throughout Jewish history have been those of men, seen through the perspective of men's concerns. Although women played important roles within that context, Jewish feminists began to envision what the world would be like if women had the power to develop a Judaism based on their own perspectives and experience.

We did this knowing full well that there were many feminists (many born Jewish) who were critical of Judaism (and the other world religions) because they were based on rules defined by men. But our goal was to reclaim our traditions. We imagined how women might have addressed traditional questions and asked new ones of our own. Some Jewish feminists identified with the traditional denominations (Orthodox, Conservative, and Reform) and organizations (National Council for Jewish Women, Hadassah) and sought to engage them and integrate a feminist perspective. Others rejected the standard versions of Judaism and found homes in Renewal, Havurah, Reconstructionist, Secular, or Humanist Judaism that developed along with the feminist movement and were more amenable to feminism from the beginning. Working within and outside the institutional structures, Jewish women have made innovations. We have challenged laws on marriage and divorce, created new prayers and celebrations, demanded leadership positions (except for the Orthodox, all denominations of Judaism have ordained women as rabbis for over twenty years), and written new interpretations of old traditions (or feminist *midrash*). Jewish feminists have also made contributions to issues that matter to the secular feminist movement such as workplace equity, domestic violence, sexual assault, and reproductive rights, using Jewish texts and traditions to inform Jewish communities about the importance of these issues and to support gender justice in the secular world.

RITUAL AND *MIDRASH*

The problems all started with Eve. The second biblical story of creation has been used throughout Jewish (and Christian) history to justify second-class status for women. According to the standard reading of the story, Eve encourages Adam to disobey God's command and is punished accordingly. She and all women forever after suffer pain in childbirth. But more, as it says in Genesis, she is "cursed": "Your desire shall be for your husband and he shall rule over you." Seeing pain in childbirth as God's command makes sense as an ancient society's effort to offer a reason for the otherwise inexplicable fact that childbirth is indeed excruciating. Although heterosexual women might ponder why desiring one's husband is a curse, our real concern is how this text makes male domination (here in marriage but surely also in society) the norm.

Jewish (and Christian) feminists found several ways to deal with the problem. Some, of course, decided that Judaism (and Christianity) should be abandoned for more woman-friendly religions, and got involved in Wicca and other forms of goddess worship. Others took a scholarly approach and tackled the text, finding more user-friendly translations and interpretations of the story. Jewish feminist theologian Judith Plaskow came up with a midrashic solution. She knew that the ancient rabbis, perplexed that there were two creation stories in Genesis, invented two wives for Adam: Lilith, to be Adam's wife in the first story, and Eve in the revised version. The rabbis suggested that Lilith was also disobedient in her own way, insisting on equality with Adam, and so was banished. God had to start all over, hence the need for two stories. In Jewish folklore, Lilith becomes an angry demon who kills babies in revenge. For Plaskow, this story created new possibilities. What if Lilith was a hero and not a demon? Plaskow imagined Lilith's return to the Garden and her subversive conversations with Eve, another disobedient woman, and the rest was Jewish feminist history. An avalanche of *midrash* followed, reimagining the thoughts and deeds of biblical women. What was Sarah thinking when her husband planned to sacrifice his son? Might Ruth have been attracted to Naomi? What about Jephthah's (unnamed) daughter—what was she doing in the months prior to her death, which was brought on by her father's vow? And why did we forget Miriam's powerful role as poet and leader during the Exodus?

The creation of ritual was also an important part of the process of creating a feminist Judaism. Giving women an equal role in life cycle ceremonies was a first step. Jewish feminists rethought the wedding ceremony and changed the language of the vows (women didn't say anything in the traditional ceremony). We reworked the marriage contract (*ketubah*), which included discussions of how much a virgin was worth. We added a ceremony to welcome baby girls that was parallel to the *bris* (covenant of circumcision) for boys where there was none before. We insisted that girls have coming-of-age ceremonies equivalent to the Bar Mitzvah (the Bat Mitzvah). We also changed holiday celebrations: injecting feminist ritual (Miriam's cup, the orange on the *seder* plate) at Passover, rethinking the role of Esther at Purim, reclaiming the celebration of Rosh Hodesh (the new moon) as a woman's holiday.

The more daring ones challenged Jewish theology, too, and questioned God's maleness. The God of the Hebrew Bible, after all, isn't made in a human image. God doesn't have a sex, so why refer to God with male pronouns and attributes such as king and warrior? While Jewish feminist theologians never actually changed the words of the Bible itself, they did write new liturgy using female or gender-neutral God language and changed the way many Jews imagine and pray to God. The ubiquitous Hebrew liturgical phrase *melech ha olam* became "ruler of the world" instead of "king of the universe," or else changed into *mkor ha hayim* (source of life) instead.

Jewish laws excluded women from other aspects of ritual life. We have either fought to change or found ways to circumvent Jewish law in order to count in a Jewish prayer quorum (*minyan*), to be called to say blessings during the reading of Torah (*aliyah*), to lead a *seder* or the blessings after meals, to be counted as witnesses for legal contracts, and to be relied upon as experts in legal and ritual matters. We have also made changes that were not against Jewish law but simply contravened custom, such as allowing women to perform as cantors and rabbis, say *kaddish* for a dead parent, learn in *yeshivah*, read publicly from the Torah scroll, and pray with ritual garb (*tallis, tefillin, kippah*). None of these inequalities was based on law or aversion to women's menstrual cycles, as popular opinion presumed.

Not everyone understands the deep connection between ritual change and justice, but feminist Judaism has made a difference through them. Those in authority took notice and incorporated these changes. It also didn't hurt that women were gaining authority in their own right and consequently could make some of the changes themselves. Making sure we're included in a visible way in the ritual life of the Jewish people encourages us to see ourselves as agents of change. These reimagined stories and new rituals gave Jewish women strong role models and a way of seeing themselves as valued actors in Jewish life. These, in turn, empowered us to continue the process of seeking justice within Jewish life on other fronts for women.

DIVORCE

Jewish feminists have tangled with religious authorities on a most serious problem—Jewish divorce. Although divorce is legal in Judaism, and both men and women can claim to be the injured party, the legal ceremony can be initiated only by the husband. Practically speaking, in communities that follow Jewish law (Orthodox communities around the world and all Jews in Israel) women can find themselves in a situation where they cannot remarry even after they are separated because their husband refuses to do the paperwork to give the woman a *get*—the document that will allow her to marry again. In some more liberal circles, where *tzedek* is compromise rather than a strict interpretation of the law, the marriage contract contains a clause that gives a court permission to act in the husband's stead, should he refuse later on. The problem can also be solved if a rabbinic court takes on the authority to grant the divorce in any case. However, some judges have been unwilling to do that, and the woman in question becomes an *agunah*, literally "chained woman." Often these cases involve domestic violence and a husband's refusal to grant a *get* is extortion and abuse. Jewish women have organized social and legal support systems for *agunot* and campaign for relief from the system.

JEWISH FEMINISTS AND WOMEN'S ISSUES

It is impressive to see how much change has taken place within the Jewish community to address women's inequality and create gender justice. So many of these changes have become a routine part of Jewish life that today they are taken for granted. Of course, not every problem is solved. Gender parity in terms of high levels of leadership is still a problem in the Jewish community. Major organizations and rabbinical schools have almost exclusively male leadership, and a wage gap still exists in most Jewish communal jobs. By and large, however, achieving gender justice in the Jewish community is a story of success.

Jewish feminists have also been involved in bringing issues from the secular feminist agenda to a Jewish audience. Jewish women's groups have been involved in working against trafficking in women. Prostitution is legal in Israel, and in and around Tel Aviv are a great number of brothels and massage parlors. Many of the women who do sex work do so willingly. However, others find themselves doing this work because conditions in their home countries (primarily the former Soviet Union) have compelled them to find avenues of escape. Too often those avenues include organized crime. Young women are helped to emigrate and sold into prostitution, often receive no salary, and labor under terrible working conditions and ill-treatment, including rape and abuse.

Jewish feminists have raised the issue of domestic violence in the Jewish community. For many years, Jewish community leaders believed that violence was not a problem among Jews. However, several groups organized to raise awareness of this problem. In the United States and Israel, Jewish feminist organizations sponsor programs that provide emotional support and legal options for Jewish women and men who experience violence in their homes. These efforts also include public programs such as the Anti-Domestic Violence Sabbath, during which rabbis are urged to give sermons and conduct special study sessions on the topic. These anti-violence groups send out literature and materials to educate rabbis about the seriousness and breadth of this problem. They also make stickers available to place in women's restrooms in synagogues. These stickers give the local domestic violence hotline number so that women can obtain information in privacy.

Sexual violence in the Jewish community is also on the Jewish feminist agenda. Although rape is a crime in the Hebrew Bible, the traditional texts don't offer sophisticated perspectives on these issues. The Awareness Center of the Jewish Coalition Against Sexual Abuse/Assault provides mechanisms to train rabbis to counsel survivors and perpetrators. It also makes advice available to adult survivors of childhood sexual abuse on how to deal with difficult family situations at critical times such as Jewish holidays.

Jewish feminists have also worked for increased access to family planning, despite mixed messages in Jewish tradition. Birth control is strictly regulated in Jewish canonical texts. Acts of birth control that block or thwart seminal emission (such as coitus interruptus or condoms) are not permitted. The birth control pill, which does not block semen at all, provided a simple solution to the problem of thwarting seminal emission and is considered the most appropriate form of birth control in traditional Jewish circles. However, the use of condoms is now allowed in order to fight sexually transmitted diseases because the value of *pikuah nefesh*, or "saving a life," supersedes all other considerations in Jewish tradition.

Medieval texts contain extensive discussions about whether certain categories of women, such as those who are prepubescent or nursing, are permitted or required to use a *mokh* (a cloth inserted in the vagina similar to a diaphragm). Commentators disagree about whether the text is saying that they *may* do this, in which case it is permissible for others as well, or that they *must* do this, meaning it is required for only these categories of women and that therefore others may not use this form of contraception. Either way, this text clearly established a warrant for birth control based on the particular situation of the woman and the well-being of children who are already born (who would suffer, presumably, if a woman became pregnant while nursing).

Demographic questions have always been an important factor in determining Jewish attitudes toward birth control. In the Talmud, some authorities suggest that two children are sufficient, while a minority opinion holds that a couple must have one child of each sex to fulfill the commandment to "be fruitful and multiply" (although technically Jewish law obligates only men to fulfill this commandment, an odd twist). During times of plague and destruction, rabbinic leaders encouraged Jews to have more children. A new openness to bringing in converts through intermarriage or choice has increased Jewish numbers to some extent, but still, in current times, Jews are encouraged to have children for several reasons. The Jewish people in the twentieth century endured the decimation of one-third of their total population as a result of the Holocaust. Living in open societies has led to opportunities for personal freedom, assimilation, and intermarriage, all of which have decreased the Jewish population.

The Orthodox community takes this quite seriously, and large families tend to be the norm. In liberal communities, many people are satisfied with fulfilling the minimal commandment of having two children, while others, concerned about population growth, may not have children at all. As usual, Jews have many opinions on this subject. Those who are deeply engaged in environmentalism aren't willing to exempt themselves or the Jewish people from the necessity to limit population in response to the worldwide crisis. They believe those of us who live in the resource-rich areas of the world must take responsibility for the intolerable lives of many who go without clean air, arable land, potable water, and sufficient food while we consume beyond our fair share of those resources. Birth control is certainly not the only way to solve the population crisis, but it can't be disregarded. Groups such as the Religious Action Center of Reform Judaism represent Jewish interests on this topic; they lobby Congress to increase funding for Title IX and encourage individuals to advocate for an end to the ban on funding international family planning.

JUDAISM AND ABORTION

For North Americans today, the most controversial gender justice issue is the question of abortion. While there is no one Jewish view of abortion, Jewish views are quite distinct from those of other religions on this subject. Ancient Jewish texts never dealt with the question of abortion as an issue of choice. All the texts focus on situations in which the life of the mother is endangered. Nonetheless, contemporary thinkers draw on these texts to support various Jewish views of abortion. More traditional segments of the Jewish community, of course, define the acceptable circumstances for abortion more narrowly than do liberal ones. However, all readings of Jewish texts suggest that abortion is neither equivalent to murder, since the fetus is always only a potential life, nor a method of birth control, the use of which is to be determined exclusively by the needs or desires of the woman who is carrying that fetus. The rejection of extremes—abortion as murder or abortion as absolute choice—is quite helpful in the polarized discussion today on this subject. Jewish tradition encourages us to look for a compromise, reminding us that often justice (*tzedek*) can be promoted through an open exchange of ideas.

Many people assume that because so much anti-abortion rhetoric emanates from religious sources, this position must be biblically based. But that's not the case. The only reference to abortion in the Hebrew Bible concerns a woman whose fetus is killed because someone strikes her and causes her to abort as an unintended consequence. The concern of the legal text in which this question arose was whether or not the person who hit the woman committed a capital crime by killing the fetus. The biblical writers concluded that it is not a capital crime and that the person who struck her owes her husband monetary compensation for the loss of property only.

The most important Jewish text about abortion is found in the Mishnah (the legal text at the core of the Talmud). It states that if at the time of birth the fetus is threatening the life of the woman carrying it, the fetus may be dismembered and killed in order to save the woman's life. The fetus is thought of as a *rodef* (pursuer). A *rodef* need not be a person; the term is also used to refer to luggage that must be thrown overboard to save those imperiled on a sinking ship. The word comes from the same root as in the biblical command to pursue (*tirdof*) justice, a word that signifies a powerful force. Many commentators read this text as suggesting that when a woman experiences the fetus as a threat to her well-being, emotional or physical, at any point during the pregnancy, abortion is justified. Others have argued that the verse means that abortion is acceptable in Judaism only if the woman's life is in danger and only at the time of birth.

There are other texts that support a more expansive reading of the text in the Mishnah. They give evidence that Judaism's primary concern is the mother's health and wishes. Another passage in the Mishnah states that if a pregnant woman is herself convicted of a capital crime, the fetus should be aborted before she is executed. The rabbis reason that she should not be executed while she is pregnant to avoid causing her unnecessary embarrassment. She should also not be forced to wait until she gives birth to be executed so as not to prolong her suffering. Since by the time this text was codified Jews did not have the authority to perform state acts of killing, this was a hypothetical case, as are many cases in the Talmud. However, it does give us an idea of the workings of the ancient rabbinic mind-set on this subject, making it abundantly clear that the pregnant woman's needs are the focal point for decision making.

This perspective is reinforced by a medieval source that suggests that a pregnant woman should be given anything to satisfy her cravings, even if what she wants is known to cause miscarriage. It is clear from this text that the woman's needs determine whether or not abortion should take place; there is no concern that the fetus itself might be subject to harm or pain.

While arguments that favor the needs of the mother make a strong case in favor of Jewish support for abortion, there are limits. There is no room in Jewish teaching for ending a pregnancy because the fetus is either carrying a disease or the wrong sex or simply isn't wanted. There is no such thing as a wrongful life. A fetus known as a result of amniocentesis to have Down syndrome or Tay-Sachs disease could not be aborted according to Jewish teaching. However, if a woman really believes that she is incapable of raising a child with severe disabilities and she is convinced that carrying the pregnancy to term would threaten her in some profound way, abortion is indeed an option that can be considered.

Looking at these texts, we can assume that Judaism takes a strong pro-choice position. It's quite clear that Jewish traditional texts don't engage in the contemporary debate that pits the woman's needs against a fetus's right to life. The fetus simply did not have needs or rights. A fetus was not a person until birth. For forty days after conception, the fetus was "mere water," and a part of the woman throughout gestation. Birth was the beginning of life, but even birth was not an absolute marker of one's personhood. One didn't bury a baby that died before it was a month old. And there's some fanciful rabbinic discussion that suggested that a child may not have had a soul until he or she learned to talk.

Abortion is a perfect example of why we can't rely solely on ancient texts to deal with contemporary problems. The ancient sources were no more enlightened on the subject of abortion than they were about homosexuality. Contemporary discussions of both subjects reflect changes in cultural awareness and advances in scientific knowledge and ethical thinking. What distinguishes progressive approaches to religion is an acknowledgment that things change. While we actively seek to connect to what our ancestors thought, we must also think for ourselves and trust our own judgment about the implications of new knowledge.

What has changed in our times is a growing sensibility that the fetus, although less than a human, is more than "mere water." Most people find it difficult to look at fetal photography and not be moved by how alive a fetus is or to be with a pregnant woman who wants to give birth to the fetus she is carrying and to sense her connection to it. We cannot be as glib as the ancient rabbis at the loss of a potential life. We must acknowledge that abortion is ending a potential life, and in that sense it is killing.

Killing, however, must be differentiated from murder. The rabbinic depiction of the fetus as *rodef*, a pursuer, is most helpful here. We are allowed to kill pursuers in self-defense, and a woman who is pregnant but didn't choose to be must ask herself whether she is acting justly in wanting to terminate the pregnancy. If the fetus is a threat to the woman, however she construes it, abortion is a justifiable alternative. If, however, the fetus is not a threat and the woman can't claim that she is defending herself against it, the fetus has a right to continue its growth into a person. But it is the woman who has the responsibility to decide whether and what kind of threat she experiences from the fetus. Jewish tradition teaches that women are allowed to use birth control because a woman is not obligated to build the world by harming herself. While abortion should not be understood as birth control per se, the same reasoning does apply. From a Jewish justice perspective this choice should not be made casually. The woman must really consider this with great seriousness and, if possible, consult with others whom she trusts to help her make this weighty decision. Under no circumstances, however, should the state make this decision for her. Jewish tradition respects mothers and their decision-making capacities.

Once the decision is made a woman needs to be able to carry it out in safety. Jews who pursue justice work for safe, legal abortion and are on record as supporting a woman's right to choose, as are most major Jewish organizations. Nineteen Jewish organizations are members of the Religious Coalition for Reproductive Choice. That's an astonishing half (give or take) of the forty-one organizations that are members of this organization, and a broad representation of the organized Jewish community: Conservative, Reconstructionist, Humanist, and Reform Judaism; women's groups such as Hadassah, Na'amat, and the National Council of Jewish Women; and secular organizations such as the American Jewish Congress and the Anti-Defamation League. You can find the list at http://www.rcrc.org/about/members.cfm.

The Religious Coalition not only supports safe, legal abortion but views the need for abortion rights in the context of other issues of reproductive health and social justice. According to its stated mission:

Our rational, healing perspective looks beyond the bitter abortion debate to seek solutions to pressing problems such as unintended pregnancy, the spread of HIV/AIDS, inadequate health care and health insurance, and the severe reduction in reproductive health care services. We support access to sex education, family planning and contraception, affordable child care and health care, and adoption services as well as safe, legal, abortion services, regardless of income. We work for public policies that ensure the medical, economic, and educational resources necessary for healthy families and communities that are equipped to nurture children in peace and love.[1]

These issues form the true fabric of gender justice, defined as adequate health care services for everyone: men, women, and those who identify themselves as transgender in a society where all children are not only wanted but adequately cared for. Jewish members of the Religious Coalition don't only go on record as officially supporting reproductive choice. They also publish articles and legislative alerts, speak publicly in forums, and encourage their members to visit their legislators and to vote.

While national organizations play a strategic role in the effort to maintain reproductive choice, smaller groups of Jewish women have also been involved. Some have been visible in the effort to defend abortion clinics against the protests that try to disrupt their functioning. They have also

incorporated ritual into that effort, in keeping with the role
ritual plays for Jewish feminists.

For many years I participated in clinic defense with a
group of Jewish women. The clinic performed abortions very
early on Saturday mornings. Before we went to synagogue
for Sabbath services (or sometimes instead of going to synagogue) we gathered at the clinic. We escorted women past
the graphic posters and angry shouts of the protestors
(mostly male) who were trying to persuade them not to enter
the clinic. Many of the women we escorted were visibly
shaken; others were angry. In those few moments walking together, we learned their stories. They were mostly women
with other children who simply could not afford to care for
more, or women whose prior pregnancies had been difficult
to endure and who were in no position to attempt another, or
women whose birth control had failed them. Almost without
exception, they had traveled a long way because many clinics
had closed down, unable to withstand the protests and
threats of violence. The women had all thought long and
hard about going ahead with the abortion. They were outraged and hurt that those who protested thought they had
the right to intimidate or decide for them.

As we listened to the protestors week after week for
hours at a time, we too were outraged and hurt by the insults
hurled not only at the women entering the clinic but also at
us. It was the policy of our group and the clinic not to respond to the protestors directly. But it was clear to us that we
needed to take some measures to bolster ourselves, and so a

ritual was born. Each morning when we gathered we sang and prayed, chanting ancient Hebrew prayers for peace, calming ourselves for the work. It turned out to be an important part of what we did—claiming religious grounding for our viewpoint just as the protestors did for theirs.

The ritual made it clear: our beliefs empowered us to do the political work we were doing. In that, we were no different from the protestors. From this experience, we gained the insight that although we stood on opposite sides of this debate, we both took our positions from deeply held religious beliefs. Rather than experiencing only anger at the protestors, we found this effort helped us understand their humanity and their passion, even as we disagreed. Only if we can look the other in the face can we begin to find ways to work together to achieve our ultimate goal of providing all children with the emotional and material support they need to grow into healthy adults, a goal that Carlton Veazey of the Religious Coalition expressed in the group's mission statement so eloquently. That is the true goal of the justice we pursue and why we support, from a Jewish perspective, a woman's right to safe, legal abortion. And that is why gender justice is more than an unusual juxtaposition of words—it is a lifelong commitment.

3

Race

If you think Jewish racial identity is a simple matter, think again. Today, in North America, people generally assume Jews are white. Tell that to the student who took my course on race in America and assumed when authors referred to white people they didn't mean her because she was Jewish. Or consider the several young women of Chinese ancestry who celebrated their B'not Mitzvah in my synagogue this past year; or my dear friend Curtis Caldwell, the rabbi of the Israelite congregation in Newark, New Jersey; or the vast number of Jews in Israel whose families came from Algeria, Iraq, and Egypt and who think of themselves (proudly) as Arab.

Jews come in all races. But are Jews also a separate race, as my student who rejected her white identity perhaps assumed? Clearly, Adolf Hitler thought so, as did the European pseudo-scientists who called us Semites. From them, we learned the dangers of racial classifications. When differences in hair, skin, feet, and eyes get measured and whole cultures are judged more or less worthwhile accordingly, the results are cruel and unjust. Jews do know from painful experience what it's like to be cast at the bottom of a racial hierarchy. Perhaps that's what makes some Jews resist any racial designation and prefer to talk about Judaism as a religion, more like Christianity or Islam than black or white.

Yet it's clear that while Judaism may be defined as a religion, you don't have to belong to a synagogue or believe in God to be a Jew. Jewishness is a more complex identity that incorporates a sense of belonging often tribal in nature. My Jewish friends used to tell me that it was surely some Cossack who gave me my blue eyes and small nose, so comfortable were they with the idea that Jews carry a genetic imprint that makes Jewish eyes brown and noses large. Or perhaps their discomfort with the possibility that we wear our Jewishness on and in our bodies and our genetic coding caused them to joke. We Jews have always experienced tension and lack of clarity around how we define ourselves as a group. We have also experienced confusion about how much who we are is about biology and how much is about religion and culture. We recognize that what makes us Jewish is a shared history, but do we carry that history in our genes or our traditions?

The answer must be both. As science becomes more comfortable with the idea that "nature" and "nurture" interact to make us who we are, so Jews are beginning to accommodate ourselves to understanding how our genetic and social identities interact to define us. Jewish identity is some interesting combination of genes, religion, and culture that collect in populations that define themselves as Jewish. So it shouldn't have come as a surprise when genetic scientists discovered that a South African tribe known as the Lemba who proudly claim Jewish ancestry shared a distinct genetic similarity (aptly called the Cohen haplotype) to Ashkenazi, Sephardi, and Mizrachi Jewish populations.

Jews from all over the world may share a genetic heritage, but without a commitment to Jewish culture, it wouldn't mean very much. Over the millennia, and particularly in modern times, we have welcomed people from every background who want to practice Jewish religion or become a member of the Jewish tribe. And we have traveled and traded around the world, so there are Jewish populations in over 120 countries and on every continent. Given all that mixing, Jews can resist a singular racial identity because Jews, however we define ourselves, have as many genetic backgrounds as we have opinions.

But even if Jews are not one race, we can't opt out of the conversation about race today. We can agree with the widely held idea that race is not a biological category, but we live in a world that is defined socially by race. We are never simply Jews. Racism may allow Jews who are white (the Jewish majority) to benefit from being part of the majority culture; that is the very nature of privilege. Jews of African, Asian, or Middle Eastern descent have a different perspective. Their Jewish identity is always combined with a racial marker. Those who pursue justice must confront racism both inside the Jewish community and in society at large.

White justice-seeking Jews have been involved in anti-racist work in the United States since the beginning of the twentieth century, before we were perceived as white. The story of our commitment springs from the ways anti-Semitism defined the American Jewish experience. Although anti-Semitism existed in America prior to the late nineteenth century, it was not a major concern. There were a mere half million Jews in America, primarily of German and Central European descent, many of whom had amassed considerable wealth. They created Reform synagogues that accorded with Christian assumptions about how to practice religion, and comported themselves like "Americans." But anti-Semitic feeling grew precipitously as a result of the huge numbers of Eastern European Jews who entered the country beginning in 1880 and ending in 1920. At that time, nativist sentiment closed the borders to these and other "foreigners," namely, the tired, poor, huddled masses from eastern and southern Europe.

The influx of Eastern European Jews to urban areas on the northeastern seaboard changed the character of Jewish life in the United States. These immigrants brought with them their ideas about many things. They had more traditional modes of worship and practice. They needed synagogues of their own, as they hardly recognized Reform services of the time. Organs and choirs, rabbis in robes, collection plates passed, and the Sabbath observed on Sundays just wasn't what they were used to. They also brought commitments to such foreign ideas as socialism, the labor movement, Yiddish culture, and Zionism that had developed in their Eastern European world. German Jews, who called themselves Hebrews or Israelites most of the time, had little in common with these immigrants, yet in this country the majority Christian population viewed them all as Jews. And Jews, like other immigrant groups of the era, did not qualify as white. Discomfited by the changing character of the American Jewish community, the German Jews provided economic and cultural assistance for the immigrants, as much because they wanted them to assimilate as because of any sense of obligation to their "co-religionists," although both motives likely obtained.

The German Jews also created organizations of Jewish self-defense to combat rising anti-Semitism. The nativist posture that inspired restrictions on immigration in the 1920s marked the beginning of an era of virulent anti-Semitism that continued through World War II. This period included anti-Semitic violence, hate groups, and publicly prominent men such as Henry Ford, Father Coughlin, and Gerald L.K. Smith, who openly preached anti-Jewish hate. Rumors abounded about Jews' insufficient loyalty to the United States. Accusations proliferated about international Jewish conspiracies in which Jews were envisioned simulta-neously as capitalists, as Bolsheviks, and as cowards evading the draft.

In addition to attending to anti-Semitism, the German and Eastern European Jews were also involved in combating anti-Black racism. Many theories have been advanced to sug-gest why so many Jews were so deeply committed to foster-ing the legal rights and integration of African Americans throughout the first half of the twentieth century. The com-mitment to justice that is deeply ingrained in Jewish textual tradition and in the theology of a just God who will deliver the oppressed from bondage played an important role. Jews took to heart how important the biblical Exodus is in the mythology of both groups, and strongly identified with the Black American experience of slavery based on the Passover story, which tells every Jew that he or she personally must experience Passover as if redeemed from slavery.

Jews also understood the oppression of African Americans because of anti-Semitism and often drew parallels between these experiences. But scholars also see a variety of motives that had to do not only with altruism but also with communal self-preservation. Some suggest that Jews subscribed to the "unitary theory of bigotry." This theory suggests that in order to end one form of oppression, all oppression will have to be eradicated. So a fight against anti-Semitism would, by definition, include working against all forms of racial and ethnic injustice.

Fighting against racism also helped the Jews maintain their identity in the face of assimilation. The dream of equality that the Enlightenment had promised the Jews had finally come to pass. But the bargain of the Enlightenment came at a price: for individual freedom, Jews had to struggle to maintain their cultural identity. In exchange for equality, Jews were expected to assimilate. One way Jews could justify their existence as a distinct cultural group was by fighting for the rights of others. As Murray Friedman suggested, "work for a society in which economic disadvantage and intolerance would have no place became a religio-cultural obsession."[1] In the fight for integration, Blacks became surrogates for Jews in the Jewish mind.

Most historians date the first organized public efforts of the Jews in America to fight against bigotry to the lynching of

Leo Frank, a southern Jew, in 1915. This event heightened Jewish awareness of the lynching of Blacks and also made Jewish leaders realize that something had to be done to combat acts of violence against both Blacks and Jews. American Jewish historian Hasia Diner emphasized how in the first part of the twentieth century Jews of all types, at least in the North, championed the African American cause. Distinguished Jewish leaders including Stephen Wise, Lillian Wald, Emil Hirsch, Louis Marshall, and Felix Frankfurter all signed the call that would result in the founding of the NAACP in 1909, professing their belief in extending full equality to African Americans. Philanthropists such as Jacob Schiff, Lessing Rosenwald, and Felix Warburg (the same German Jews who funded the acculturation of the Eastern European immigrants) gave unstintingly to historically Black colleges and were the financiers of the major African American civil rights institutions: the NAACP, the Urban League, and the Congress of Racial Equality. Jewish and Black leaders formed an alliance to pass New Deal reforms, including increased bargaining rights for unions. Jews in the Communist Party championed Paul Robeson and fought for integration. Only the Jews of the South, who found themselves comfortably allied with southern life as it existed under Jim Crow, were not part of this developing consciousness.[2]

World War II brought about major changes for minority groups in the United States. Fighting fascism abroad shed a new and negative light on segregation and hatred at home. How could we as a society object to Hitler's racist policies against the Jews and other groups in Europe if we practiced the same kind of racial politics against Jews, Blacks, and others right here in America? The war made it obvious to many, especially the young men and women returning from the war, that change was necessary. Before the war, institutional discrimination was the norm, and bigotry in the form of verbal slurs and separate spaces was not only tolerated but presumed. World War II marked an end to virulent and public anti-Semitism. Jews (and other European immigrants) became more acceptable. Karen Brodkin, in her book *How Jews Became White Folks and What That Says About Race in America*, argues that the GI Bill created the most important opportunities for Jewish assimilation.

Jews, however, continued to assume a deep connection between themselves and Blacks that obscured the real differences of mid-twentieth-century America. It was becoming clear that although this new tolerance meant two different things for Jews and Blacks, Jews (and some Blacks as well) wanted to believe that their successes were also possible for African Americans. They saw in America the potential for tolerance based on their own experiences and did not discern any difference between anti-Black racism and anti-Semitism. They were proud to have been part of the fight against bigotry from the beginning of the twentieth century onward. Jews tended to ignore the aspects of our story in America that put us in conflict with Blacks, such as the roles Jews played as merchants, landlords, and employers of Black domestic labor, in both the North and the South.

The Jewish commitment to achieving full integration for Blacks and our self-image as fellow victims of bigotry fueled

Jewish participation in and support of the civil rights movement. Jewish leaders were prominently involved in marches and demonstrations, and Jews participated as Freedom Riders in voter registration drives of the early 1960s. This broad-based commitment ended by 1965 when the rise of the Black power movement, a new focus on affirmative action, and the Black community's support of the Palestinians after 1967 brought greater tension to this complex relationship. Incidents of anti-Semitism on the part of Blacks and conflicts over integration in housing and community control of the schools were highly publicized in the media. Over time, the idea that a special relationship had ever existed between Blacks and Jews came to be seen as mostly a product of Jewish desire and imagination.

And yet Black-Jewish collaborations based on this historic alliance continue. The Black and Jewish lobbying groups and congressional caucuses work together often around shared domestic priorities. Prominent Black and Jewish progressives such as Michael Lerner and Cornel West publish books such as *Jews and Blacks: A Dialogue on Race, Religion and Culture in America.* And groups such as Operation Understanding, created by the American Jewish Committee and the Urban League, bring together youth from Black and Jewish backgrounds to study and travel in an effort to create cross-cultural understanding.

Still, much of the notion that the relationship between Blacks and Jews is something unique or special comes from justice-seeking Jews who express their commitment to anti-racism work in a variety of ways. Jewish museums sponsor exhibits such as "Bridges and Boundaries" that explore Black-Jewish relationships.[3] Jews celebrate their historical connection to supporting Jackie Robinson and the integration of baseball. Many Jewish communities honor the relationship between Abraham Joshua Heschel and Martin Luther King Jr. on the Shabbat before Martin Luther King Jr. Day each January. These celebrations are ritually based, but also include an examination of contemporary Black-Jewish connections. Speakers from Black churches and other groups are often invited, and sometimes these celebrations will include involvement in acts of justice or community service.

Yachad (Hebrew for "together"), the Jewish Community Housing Development Corporation of Washington D.C., raises funds and organizes volunteers from the Jewish community. The volunteers participate in activities such as renovating church buildings in the Black community that will become housing for homeless families. The volunteers work and eat with members of the church. The goal is not only community service but also the creation of dialogue between Blacks and Jews, intended to end anti-Black racism.[4]

Jews for Racial and Economic Justice (JFREJ) has been engaged in anti-racism work since its inception in 1992. It was involved in the (successful) efforts to resist privatization of New York's public schools, where the majority are students of color. The organization led Jewish efforts to fight police brutality and was deeply involved in the fight to bring to justice the police officers responsible for Guinean immigrant Amadou Diallo's death. Their current effort is in support of the rights of domestic workers, mostly immigrant women of color, to a living wage, benefits, and better working conditions.

Racial justice is an important component of the agenda of Jewish Community Action in Minneapolis and St. Paul. In addition to working on issues such as affordable housing, JCA sponsors a Racial Justice Working Group that provides anti-racism training sessions, technical assistance, and curricula for members of the Minneapolis/St. Paul Jewish community.

The Jewish Council on Urban Affairs in Chicago was founded in 1964 by Jewish civil rights leaders. Recognizing the enduring legacy of racism, they have continued their mission of working with the African American community on issues including affordable housing, education reform, the creation of community gardens, and voter registration in low-income, segregated communities.

Through these and many other efforts, Jews seek justice on behalf of African Americans, predicated on the assumption that Jews are white. And there is no doubt that the majority of the Jews in the world today would be included in that categorization. Ashkenazi Jews (those Yiddish speakers who come from countries in northern and eastern Europe) make up about 80 percent of the total U.S. Jewish population, which numbers around 6 million.[5] But Jews who seek justice must also value the experiences and viewpoint of the 20 percent.

To be clear, the other 20 percent of Jews aren't exclusively of African descent. They also include Sephardi Jews who trace their ancestry back to the Iberian Peninsula and whose ancestors probably spoke Ladino (Judeo-Spanish). Many Sephardim live in Israel today, but many also reside in Latin America. Latin America is also home to considerable numbers of Ashkenazi Jews who arrived there from Europe at one point or another, many fleeing the Holocaust. The Sephardim were the first Jews to arrive in the western hemisphere, and the first to live in the American colonies as well. Some fleeing the Inquisition in 1492 had formally converted to Christianity while maintaining Jewish practice. They were called *conversos.* Some rediscovered their Jewish origins centuries later.

Mizrachi Jews (sometimes lumped together with Sephardim) are also part of the 20 percent. They come from North Africa and the various countries that constituted the old Ottoman Empire, or the Middle East. Their ancestors spoke Judeo-Arabic. There are also Jewish communities in India, China, and many other countries in Asia. While Jews from these communities have migrated to North America, many more reside in Israel, although a small number remain in their countries of origin.

African-heritage Jews are also a mixed multitude. Some are African Americans who converted to Judaism through conviction or marriage (quite common during the civil rights movement) and their children and grandchildren. White Jewish families adopted others. African Americans also found Judaism through teachers and leaders who saw an affinity between their ancient African heritage and Judaism, and created communities today known as Black Hebrew or Israelite. White Jews encouraged some of those communities to convert to Ashkenazi religious practices, while others maintained their own distinct Jewish traditions. Some Afro-Caribbean and African American Jews may trace their heritage back to the times of slavery, when Jewish plantation owners made them (or permitted them to, depending on your perspective) become Jewish, although how common this experience was is also, not surprisingly, the subject of much controversy. And we are discovering a large number of Africans who practice Judaism as well. The communities of Ethiopia (Beta Yisrael) and South Africa and Zimbabwe (Lemba) are well known. But in recent years we also have made contact with African Jewish groups in Uganda, Kenya, and Ghana.

The presence of this large and vital part of the American Jewish community causes us to ask this question: if you are a Black Jew, then whatever does a Black-Jewish alliance or relationship mean from your perspective? With that in mind, we might begin to rethink some of the contours of what racial justice means from a Jewish perspective.

RETHINKING THE BIBLE

When white Jews imagine what our ancestors from the time of the Bible and Talmud looked like—Isaiah for example—we see in our mind's eye a man, probably dressed in some robe and bearded, courtesy of Hollywood or perhaps Renaissance art. He might be tall or short, heavy or thin, young or old. We may each cast this character differently, but likely we'd make him a swarthy-looking guy, probably on the

Mediterranean side, but most likely with Caucasian features, no doubt like the Jesus from Mel Gibson's *Passion of the Christ*. But imagine Isaiah with curly hair, a wide nose, and dark skin, and you might get closer to the real picture. That is, I'm told, how Jews of African descent see our ancestors. When white Jews think about the story of Moses' sister Miriam's distress over his marriage to a Cushite woman, as described in Exodus, we make the assumption that she was upset because the woman came from an African land and presumably had dark skin. But when Jews of African descent hear that story, they are more likely to imagine some familial squabble that has nothing to do with skin color. White Jews may not care much about the curse of Ham, Noah's son in Genesis whose progeny was punished for Ham's disrespect of his father after the flood. But for Black Jews, proving that the biblical story is not the basis for slavery and racism, as later Christian commentators assumed, is quite important. Just as those of us who care about gender justice have changed our image of God, so those of us who care about racial justice might start changing our image of prophets, kings, and rabbis.

White Jews must also think about how we react when Jews of African descent appear in predominantly white Jewish spaces. Melanie Kaye/Kantrowitz, in her important new book *The Colors of Jews*, interviews many African American Jews who tell of experiences similar to ones that friends have reported to me. When Black Jews enter a predominantly white synagogue for the first time, if they aren't ignored, they experience a barrage of questions betraying doubts about

their Jewishness. Even if they are wearing ritual garb, such as
a *tallit* or *kippah*, they are often subject to inquiries about
their Jewish identities. When they say they are Jewish, the
white Jews will more often than not ask how the Black Jews
became Jewish. (When I mention my Black Jewish acquain-
tances to white Jewish friends, I often get a similar response.)
White Jews don't do this to other white Jews. If a white person (or a person who by appearance looks to be Sephardi or
Mizrachi) says he or she is Jewish, and seems comfortable
with the prayer service, that person is a presumptive Jew,
even if he or she is not. Justice demands that white Jews make
the same assumption about the Jewishness of Black Jews.

While some Black Jews want to worship in predominantly white spaces, and others are secular and don't worship
at all, still others are more comfortable in the Israelite world.
While we have no way of knowing how many Israelites there
are, estimates number around 200,000. We do know that
there are multiple congregations in New York, Philadelphia,
Chicago, Virginia, St. Louis, New Jersey, and California, as
well as a school that trains rabbis and conducts other adult
education, the Israelite Academy, in Queens, New York.[6]
There are different denominations, and they are at the beginning stages of cooperation. They connect to each other
through the Israelite Board of Rabbis and to other "Jews of
color" through Be'chol Lashon, an initiative of the Institute
for Jewish and Community Research in San Francisco. A few
of these groups have engaged with white Jewish communal
structures. Rabbi Capers Funnye, leader of Beth Shalom
congregation in Chicago, is a member of the Chicago Board

of Rabbis and involved in Jewish multiracial conversations. Other groups have experienced rejection by the white Jewish community over the years and do not want to open lines of communication. Others have had good experiences with co-operative rabbis who have helped them get started, providing them with prayer books, Torah scrolls, and other expertise. There are also Israelite groups that have converted to Orthodox Judaism under the auspices of Ashkenazi rabbis. Sometimes that has worked out well. But in other cases even those who have converted have not been welcomed.

Another group, the African Hebrew Israelites of Jerusalem, numbers 2,000 and follows a spiritual leader, Ben Ammi. The group originated in Chicago, migrated toLiberia, and since 1969 has made its home in Dimona, Israel. After some battles with the religious leadership over their claims to Israeli citizenship based on their Jewish identity, they have found a comfortable existence there.[7]

Predominantly white Jewish congregations may accept individual "Jews of color," converts, or the children and partners of members with not much difficulty, although experiences of unconscious racism are also not uncommon. But many Ashkenazi Jews view Israelites (or Jewish groups in Africa) as "other." They are not prepared to include them in predominantly white Jewish community organizations and structures. Israelites may wish to maintain separate communal organizations, but why are the Commandment Keepers or the Church of God and Saints of Christ not treated like other denominations of American Jews? Why are they not included when we see descriptions of American Judaism in textbooks or encyclopedias or on the Internet? Their rituals and practices are unique, but no more different than Orthodox and Humanistic observances are from one another. Some of the Israelite groups see themselves as biblical Jews and don't follow rabbinic law, but then neither did Reform Judaism in the nineteenth century. Some groups do believe that Jesus was the messiah or follow the teachings of Islam in conjunction with Jewish observance. The mainstream Jewish community struggles with white Messianic Judaism and is generally uncomfortable acknowledging any of these groups as Jewish. Justice demands that we make new approaches to learn about all these groups, welcome connections where appropriate, and develop mechanisms for intrafaith dialogue.

The problem is not only about religious communities; it exists in the progressive Jewish social justice world as well. According to Melanie Kaye/Kantrowitz, even Jewish groups such as Jews for Racial and Economic Justice and the Jewish Council on Urban Affairs that have worked diligently against racism have not yet found a mechanism to connect to Jews of color. They don't yet see the relationship between their social justice work in the world and educating the Ashkenazi Jewish community about Jewish diversity. Kaye/Kantrowitz raises these questions in *The Colors of Jews* to open the dialogue in the progressive secular Jewish world.[8]

When white Jews begin to look at the world through a Black Jewish lens, we might also shift some of our priorities. We would probably feel some greater connection to and curiosity about all those who practice Judaism in sub-Saharan Africa. We might also understand the role of slavery in Jewish history in the Western Hemisphere somewhat differently as well. We would probably feel a deeper connection to all African Americans and to Africa as a land of some of our people's heritage. And when we think about Jewish social justice issues, we would most likely focus on problems in Darfur and other African countries, the racial dimension of poverty here in the United States, and the accompanying infant mortality, unemployment, credit barriers, overrepresentation in prison, and substandard education that afflict many African Americans.

But that's not enough. Whites are notorious in the Black community for our love of talk and dialogue and our desire to be friends; that's not a bad first step. But what Blacks often want and need is for us to prove our commitment through action. What action, then might be appropriate? Let's begin to pay attention to the call in the Black community for reparations for their enslavement. Ashkenazi Jews who suffered under the Nazi regime were the pioneers in this area, and Israel's economy is built on the honest efforts of Germany to pay the Jews for our unpaid labor. Poles, Japanese Americans, Inuits, and Aboriginal groups in Australia have all received the benefit of reparative justice.

The claim of African Americans is powerful and simply put: to enslave a group of people for hundreds of years (and in the process rob an entire continent of human resources), set them free without the promised forty acres and a mule, pit them against their victimizers, and continue to segregate them legally for another hundred years created a disproportionate amount of poverty (and its concomitant woes) for

African Americans. Were white Jews responsible? While we must discount the Nation of Islam's claim that Jews dominated the slave trade, we cannot ignore the fact that we were slave owners in the South until emancipation and in the North during colonial times, after which free Blacks continued to work in Jewish households as domestics. Eli Faber discovered that in the Carolinas, the 1790 census listed seventy-three Jewish households, and of those, thirty-four owned a total of 151 slaves. Similar documentation is available from census data in 1820 and 1840 and for Alabama, Louisiana, and Virginia.[9] But even if there were no white Jewish slaveholders, slave traders, or slavery enthusiasts, and even if most of us came here in the immigration from Eastern Europe in the early twentieth century, there is no doubt that, as white Americans, we have benefited from a country built on slave labor, and we owe a debt.

Justice-seeking Jews might get involved in the movement for reparations. We can:

- Support the legislation Representative John Conyers has introduced in Congress every year since 1989 and find out if our congressional representative has signed on as a co-sponsor; HR 40 calls for a study of remedies and an acknowledgment of harm.
- Support the plan that the National Coalition of Blacks for Reparations in America (N'COBRA) has suggested, to establish a private trust with the U.S. government funding programs for education and economic empowerment, and, for example, to set up

residential K–12 schools for kids in unhealthy neighborhoods and families that would help send the aca-
demically qualified to college.

- Work to identify and tax companies and individuals
that were unjustly enriched by slave labor and to send
the proceeds to the trust fund.
- Lobby to have the U.S. government make amends to
African nations through debt relief.
- Respond to James Forman's suggestion (first made
many years ago) when he interrupted a Sunday service
at Riverside Church and asked that churches and synagogues put up $5 million in reparations by thinking
about what part a congregation might play in that
process.

While much needs to be done to advance justice within
the Jewish community on the issue of race, there are hopeful
signs. Organizations such as the Jewish Multiracial Network
and Be'chol Lashon have created a support system for Jews
of color and their families and allies. The Center for Afro-
Jewish Studies at Temple University provides a location for
academic study of the connections between the African and
Jewish diasporic traditions. Photographers and filmmakers
have begun to document Jewish diversity on the principle
that one picture of Jewish diversity may indeed be worth (at
least) a thousand words.

The city of St. Louis provides us with a unique situation,
but one that could serve as a model for other communities.

St. Louis is the home of Yavilah McCoy, founder of Ayecha/ Where Do You Stand? Resource Organization. McCoy's parents converted to Orthodox Judaism and provided her and her siblings with *yeshivah* educations when they were growing up in Brooklyn. She founded Ayecha as a national organization that does outreach and training and provides curricular materials on Jewish diversity. Their training focuses both on Jewish inclusion and anti-racism.[10]

Susan Talve is the rabbi of Central Reform Congregation, the only congregation that remains in the city of St. Louis, as the rest moved to the suburbs years ago. The first description of the congregation on its Web site is "providing an inclusive home for families and individuals," and there are repeated references throughout the site to welcoming diversity.[11] In an interview with Kaye/Kantrowitz, Talve explains that she got the message right away from the "kids of color" who were registered in her Hebrew school that their experience was different. "Once they hit middle school," she explains, "they knew they had to choose between being Black and being Jewish, and they couldn't choose not to be Black, so they stopped being Jewish in their own hearts."[12] Talve wanted her congregation to be part of the solution. She called on Yavilah McCoy, who helped organize training. The congregation held workshops on dismantling racism and did internal work developing congregational leadership on the issues. They've invited leaders from the Black Jewish community, Professor Ephraim Isaac and Rabbi Capers Funnye, to speak, and sponsored a concert by the Jewish gospel singer

Joshua Nelson. They've also made contact with the local Hebrew Israelite community through mutual visits. Talve's conclusion is inspiring:

> I got the King Leader Award from the whole state. I'm an honorary AME [African Methodist Episcopalian]. All of this because I show up. Because the African American community trusts us. Because we're doing this work. And because we're here. I'm included in the work of health care, of economic justice, of police brutality. It's been amazing. Just the visuals of it. I look out now and we are integrated. We can do it. And if we can do it here in St. Louis, we can do it anywhere.[13]

Talve sets a high standard for congregational rabbis on this (and other) social justice issues, but she also makes us believe that her pursuit of justice is possible for anyone in the Jewish community who has the desire and drive to make it happen.

As white Jews such as Gary and Diane Tobin and Melanie Kaye/Kantrowitz have pointed out, expanding our notion of who is a Jew and being inclusive can only benefit the Jewish community, broadening our tent and opening our minds. But achieving what Kaye/Kantrowitz calls a "paradigm shift" in our understanding of Jewish diversity is also an issue of justice, a necessary part of the anti-racism work that justice-seeking Jews have understood to be part of our agenda.

4

War and Peace

If you grow up Jewish in the United States, there's a pretty good chance that when December rolls around, you will be celebrating Hanukkah. In a Christian society where Christmas is the default setting for all things public for the month (November, too; most places are bedecked in red and green before you even start your Thanksgiving dinner), Hanukkah is the Jewish antidote, appropriately wrapped in blue and silver to fit the seasonal consumer spirit of our time. (As an outsider to all this, I really sympathize with the Christians who want to put the Christ back in Christmas, as long as they don't insist I do, too.)

Lighting Hanukkah candles may be an adequate substitute for a tree, and eight nights of presents can compensate for lack of a Christmas morning gifting ritual. Most American Jews know the story of the miracle in ancient Israel that made a one-day supply of oil burn for eight days. They also play a game of chance with a spinning top known as a dreidel. The Hebrew letters on the dreidel probably stand for the Yiddish words that tell you how much of the pot you won, but they also represent the Hebrew words for "a great miracle happened there." In Israel, the dreidels say "a great miracle happened here." The latkes (potato pancakes) that are eaten on this holiday are there not because of the potatoes but because they are fried in oil to remind us of the miracle. Israelis also eat fried jelly doughnuts instead of potatoes, another reminder that the variety of Jewish opinions extends to eating habits, too.

But Hanukkah has a backstory, and it's quite relevant to Jewish views of war. Hanukkah served not only as an antidote to Christmas but also as the outstanding example of and justification for Jewish military might. It was a favorite holiday of the early Zionist movement. Yet for almost two thousand years Jews showed little interest in the historical event that led to the miracle they celebrated on this holiday. The ancient rabbis actually had little interest in the holiday itself—it didn't develop its popular aspects (like dreidel playing, latke eating, and gift giving) until the Middle Ages. The ancient book that records the story of the Maccabees, Hanukkah's heroes, is not even included in the Hebrew Bible. The four books of the Maccabees are tucked into the collection of biblical leftovers called the Apocrypha. The Catholic version of the Bible includes it, but the sacred texts of Jews and Protestants do not.

In their time, the Maccabees were celebrated warriors. Their military exploits against the Seleucids led to the establishment of the Hasmonean dynasty, which ruled the kingdom of Judea from 164 to 37 B.C.E. Hanukkah marks their triumphant march into Jerusalem, which ended Seleucid influence. The Maccabees purified the Temple and removed representations of Greek gods and other Hellenistic symbols. They rededicated the Temple (the word *Hanukkah* means "dedication") to the worship of the one God, YHVH. They lit the lamp, or menorah, and declared an eight-day festival, like the pilgrimage festival of Sukkot celebrated in the fall harvest season.

The ancient rabbis were opposed to celebrating military exploits, particularly those of the Hasmoneans, who became quite corrupt during their reign. So the books that told the story of the Maccabees were not canonized, and the story in the Talmud of this event and celebration focused exclusively on the rededication of the Temple, reshaped as a miracle story instead of a military success. The Talmud tells us that although this was an eight-day festival there was only enough oil to light the ceremonial lamp for one day, so the true celebration was for God's miraculous gift of oil that sustained the light, both materially and symbolically. Instead of reading the story of the Maccabees on Hanukkah, the rabbis read from the prophet Zechariah, which reminds us that battles are won "not by might, and not by power, but by my Spirit, says the Lord."

The rabbis based their attitude on the fundamental principle in the Hebrew Bible that there are two categories of wars, those commanded by God (*mitzvah*) and those that were permitted (*reshut*). Since the second kind was not obligatory, such wars were not looked on favorably. The Maccabees' war fit into the second category. So did the wars for expansion fought by King David, who, according to the book of Chronicles, was not permitted to build the Temple in Jerusalem because of the blood on his hands. In fact, permit-

ted wars could only be fought by kings, and the Talmud in-
structs us to rebel against wars that kings command if they
are not dedicated to the highest ethical values. The biblical
text also limits aggressive behaviors associated with war. A
war could not be conducted without first calling for peace.
An aggressive war could not be waged if it would cause casu-
alties of more than one-sixth of the enemy population. The
Israelites were obligated to direct their attacks only at enemies, could not completely besiege a city, and were not to cut
down trees or destroy property. To further reinforce their antipathy toward permitted war, the rabbis set limits on declar-
ing war that simply could not be met after the biblical
era—like consulting with the *urim* and *thummim*, worn by
the ancient high priest and presumably used for divination.

Wars commanded by God, however, form a significant
part of the biblical legacy and shape Jewish attitudes toward
war and peace. They were limited to two kinds. The first was
the conquest and defense of the land of Israel, and it consisted of those battles fought against the seven nations that
inhabited the land when the Israelites arrived. Another such
war was the one against the nation of Amalek. According to
the medieval commentator Rashi, these were the only commanded wars in Jewish history. Neither of these wars has
been historically documented outside the biblical text. It is
most likely that the land was actually "conquered" by collec-
tive settlement rather than the battle that's described in the
biblical story.

The second category of commanded war is self-defense.
The Talmud makes it clear that it is always a priority to de-

fend oneself against attack. As we have seen in the discussion on Jewish views of abortion, this applies on the personal level as well. Individuals are also obligated to defend themselves against a pursuer. This emphasis on self-defense keeps Judaism from being a religion of pacifism. Yet killing is permitted only in self-defense. So is giving up one's own life, except if you are ordered to commit murder, idolatry, or incest. Saving life (*pikuah nefesh*) is an overarching Jewish principle that supersedes virtually all other commands. Individuals also have options regarding participation in war. The Bible tells us that "the fearful and fainthearted" are not obligated to serve, and there are Jewish traditions that interpret that concept not as cowardliness but as compassion, a justification that has been used by Jewish conscientious objectors. So while pacifism may not be a Jewish value, war is also not favored. At best, it is a necessary evil.

Throughout most of Jewish history, this anti-militaristic attitude prevailed. Jews did not govern a state or have a standing army and were not responsible for making war, so it was not difficult to maintain this stance. Of course, Jews did fight in wars other than the one instigated by the Maccabees. They fought against Rome, against Christians during the Crusades, and on the side of Muslims in the Christian conquest of Spain. They were conscripted into various armies, and fought for both sides in most modern wars. At the same time, Jewish leaders often spoke out against war. More often than not, this anti-warrior attitude reinforced stereotypes of Jews as "fearful and fainthearted," in both the cowardly and compassionate readings of that term. Jews took after their ancestor Jacob, who, although he wrestled with God, was considered bookish compared to his brother Esau, the hunter. There were very few Jewish gladiators in ancient Rome, and Jewish men were not known to be involved in hunting or other blood sports throughout European history. Even well-known Jewish boxers were assumed to lack a killer instinct, a sentiment you find in various literary works including *The Great Gatsby.*

Those who began to develop the philosophy of Zionism in the late 1800s in Europe were very much aware of this image of the Jew and considered it a problem. They encouraged Jewish men to become more comfortable with fighting. They saw the willingness to fight as part of the obligation men would have to undertake as part of creating a "normal" Jewish society. Given the scant evidence of other Jewish fighters throughout the ages, the Maccabees had to serve as a role model. Although the Zionist movement did not at first assume that this Jewish society would be located in Palestine, that's where the pioneers went when the British government sanctioned Jewish settlement there. These pioneers envisioned themselves returning to the land their ancestors inhabited. They convinced themselves it was "a land without a people for a people without a land," despite the presence of Arabs who called this place their home and who were angry about the influx of settlers from Europe. The wholesale destruction of European Jewry during the Holocaust contributed to the image of the weak Jews who went to their deaths "like sheep to the slaughter." But it also reinforced the Zionist assertion that Jews would not survive without a territory, protected by armed forces that would never again allow Jews to be harmed by their enemies. Not surprisingly, these ideas were met initially with skepticism and hostility by most religious Jews, but with the birth of the State of Israel things changed dramatically. For the first time in two thousand years, the Jews of Israel found themselves governing a sovereign nation that was immediately under siege and in need of military protection. Although Israel was meant to be a safe haven for Jews, the new nation ironically found itself in an almost constant state of war from that moment to this one.

ISRAEL

Any examination of Jewish views of war must come to terms with the incredible shift in Jewish sensibilities the existence of the Jewish state brought about. In fact, it is impossible to read what purports to be a theoretical discussion of Jewish views of war without thinking about the steady state of war in the Middle East and the role Israel has played in it. Some portions of the organized Jewish community would like everyone to believe that all Jews support Israel, no questions asked. But the topic of Israel is no exception to the rule that if there are two Jews, they have at least three opinions.

For some, the wars fought over the years have been an example of *mitzvah*: wars that are commanded in self-defense and in conquest of the land. To others, Israel's wars are examples of *reshut*: wars for territorial expansion that are considered permissible. But in the view of those whose Judaism is predicated on the pursuit of justice, Israel's wars have sometimes, but not always, been fought in self-defense, and there is no blanket acceptance of Israel's wars under the category of *mitzvah.* Permissible war is out of the question after the biblical era. But even if it were not, Israel has broken every biblical precept about waging war, and it must be called to account for its aggressive tactics: placing cities under siege, destroying trees and property, killing too high a percentage of the enemy population, and not making every effort to call for peace.

To be sure, Israel has enemies that seek to destroy it, and some anti-Israel sentiment is thinly disguised anti-Semitism. Yet it is simply untrue that Israel is the innocent and powerless party in a one-sided conflict. Jews who criticize the government of Israel do so knowing full well that there are (at least) two sides to every story and no simple solutions to the dilemma in the Middle East. Of course Israel is not the only responsible party in this conflict. But it is our responsibility, as Jews, to scrutinize Israel's actions based on Jewish principles and to press Israel to behave in ways that are ethical, even in the face of great odds. We cannot shy away from efforts to make peace.

Just as the prophets call on us to pursue justice, the author of Psalm 44 tells us that we must "seek peace and pursue it." While justice may be within our reach if we work for it, peace is a goal that is more difficult to attain. The Hebrew word for peace, *shalom,* comes from a root that means "perfect wholeness" or "completion." *Shalom* was a messianic concept, to be achieved when the lion lies down with the lamb, to borrow another prophetic phrase. And yet *shalom* is the most common Hebrew word, used in everyday life. We use it to say hello and goodbye and to greet each other on the Sabbath. It is in the name of half the synagogues in America, including many that are called Rodef Shalom for the seekers of peace. The Jewish liturgy includes many prayers for peace. The tradition that teaches us to seek justice also demands that we work for peace.

The desire for peace has been present among Zionists from the inception of the movement. While some talked of nationhood and governance, others wanted to build a society based on the highest Jewish ethical principles where Jewish culture could flourish. We have forgotten the cultural Zionism of Ahad Ha'am, the pseudonym of Asher Ginsburg, who wanted to create a place where Jewish art, music, literature and intellect could thrive. We have forgotten the socialist Zionism of Martin Buber and Judah Magnes, who knew that this "land without a people" was inhabited by Arabs; they argued early on for a bi-national state rather than the British partition plan in the 1940s. But after the state was established in 1948, the myth of nationhood gained absolute supremacy. During these early years Israel did much good. It established itself as a partner to African nations, a refuge for Jews fleeing from Europe and North Africa, and a vital ally to the West in the Cold War. There was little or no attention paid to the situation of the non-Jewish Arabs who were removed or who chose to remain.

Although there were Zionists in Jewish populations outside of Israel, and being anti-Zionist was becoming less acceptable in the Jewish world, in those days Israel was by

no means the center of American Jewish life. As far as my
Reform synagogue in the 1950s and 1960s was concerned,
Israel did not exist. Although there were exceptions, most of
the Reform movement was in the non-Zionist camp. Israel
wasn't part of our Hebrew school curriculum—I learned
to speak Hebrew in Ashkenazi dialect, which differed from
the Hebrew adopted by Israel. My rabbi never gave a ser-
mon about Israel, and not one dime was raised to support the
new nation. All I knew of Israel was from what I read in the
newspapers or learned in social studies class in junior high
school.

In 1967 all that changed. The Six-Day War in June put
Jewish communities around the world on notice that Israel
was vulnerable but also powerful. Its military exploits in defense of its right to exist against Arab nations bent on its destruction were an instant source of pride. Almost overnight,
Israel became the focus of American Jewish life. Any group
that had previously considered itself non-Zionist quickly
changed its tune. It became impossible to imagine that Israel
was anything less than perfect, and the belief spread that the
survival of Judaism depended on what happened in this tiny
country.

To understand this for myself, I decided to spend my
junior year of college (1969) at Hebrew University in
Jerusalem. Two years after the war, I landed in a country that
had just secured its borders, having captured land from
Syria, Jordan, and Egypt. The feeling in the country was eu-
phoric, and it was impossible not to be moved by what I saw.
In Jerusalem, I visited the holy sites of Islam, Judaism, and

Christianity, all within walking distance of one another. I saw excavations of ancient sites I had read about in the Bible alongside modern museums filled with Israeli art. I lived for the summer in the Negev desert, where I picked peaches from trees that grew in the sand. I learned Israeli folk songs and dances along with the properly accented Israeli Hebrew. I heard the inspiring words of David Ben Gurion, the country's first president, who told this group of young Americans that Israel was the key to the survival of the Jewish people. It was hard not to fall in love with the place. And then they took me to Gaza.

Not many American Jews saw this side of Israel back then, and I'm still not sure what they were thinking taking a busload of us to a refugee camp. Perhaps they meant to show us the cruelty of the Egyptians, who forced their Arab neighbors to live in conditions that were not fit for human life. Girls wore woolen dresses in sweltering heat; rationed food consisted of small amounts of oil and grain, with milk only for nursing mothers and children under five, who begged us for our leftover lunches. It was hard to envision these people as the enemy. Why Israel wasn't doing anything to ameliorate these conditions in its newly occupied lands was not explained.

I began to notice that the rhetoric said what made Israel special was that Jews did all the jobs, but the construction of my building was being done by an Arab workforce. The women who cleaned our dormitories were Arab, and so were the day laborers I observed coming from East Jerusalem early in the morning. Something was just not right.

Over the course of the year I grew alienated from the militarized culture. Compared to my friends in the United States, who were protesting the war in Vietnam and burning their draft cards, no one I met in Israel thought war was evil; the soldiers were the country's heroes. I was told that Israel was the only place Jews should live, and found my liberal American version of Jewish religion subject to amusement and even occasional ridicule. I argued with my American friends who were raised on Zionism. If they were not planning to stay and make *aliyah* (become Israeli citizens), they were feeling bad about returning to the United States.

I never questioned the need for a sovereign state, for a safe and secure place where Judaism could flourish and Jews could live in peace. I could not align myself with those forces on the American left that turned against Israel, denouncing Zionism as racism after 1967. But I also assumed that Israel intended to return the land it gained during the war in exchange for peace. I never imagined an occupation that was to last for forty-plus years and change the character of the country completely. By the end of my year in Israel, I was convinced that I was destined to be an American, not an Israeli Jew. My skepticism put me out of step in the American Jewish community, however, which was becoming more and more Israel-centered.

Israel's status as an occupier was also disturbing to others in the American Jewish community. In 1973 an option was created. The organization called itself Breira, Hebrew for "alternative" or "choice." All during my year in Israel, when I asked someone why the militarism, why the hatred of Arabs, why hold on to the ill-gotten land, they would answer, "*Ayn breira*" (there is no choice). The founders of Breira thought differently. They were Conservative and Reform rabbis, many of whom were Hillel directors on college campuses; activists such as Arthur Waskow (who had already made his voice heard on this issue); socialist Zionist organizations; and young, radical Jews in the feminist and Havurah movements. Briera's story is chronicled by historian Michael Staub.[1] He suggests that its leaders wanted to create an organization that provided an alternative for Jews like me, who lived and worked inside the Jewish community. Breira placed its mission in the context of support for and love of Israel. It criticized the Israeli government's aggressive stance against its Arab neighbors and its dealings with the occupied lands.

Breira and its leaders thought they were generating controversy, but they had no expectation of the attacks that would follow from the Jewish right wing and the mainstream Jewish community. Some of the Hillel rabbis lost their jobs. Many others were censured. The Jewish Defense League and other groups intimidated and harmed Breira's leaders. The besieged organization could not sustain itself and was disbanded in 1978.

Breira sought open conversation in the American Jewish community on the issues it cared about. It was the first Jewish organization to propose a two-state solution to the Middle East conflict, at a time when the word *Palestinian* could not be uttered in the Jewish world. They were joined in 1975 by a group of Israelis who were also deeply disturbed by the annexation of land and the direction of Israel's government.

The group formed the Israeli Council for Israeli-Palestinian Peace (ICIPP).They urged Israel to negotiate with the leaders of the Palestine Liberation Organization (PLO) for a return of the West Bank and Gaza in exchange for a promise of secure borders. The leaders included prominent Zionists such as Major General Matti Peled, former member of the Labour Party Aryeh Eliav, and journalist Uri Avineri. A religious Zionist peace group with similar aims, Oz v'Shalom (Strength and Peace), also formed in 1975.

At the time of the demise of Breira in 1978, Shalom Achshav (Peace Now) was founded in Israel, the first broadbased peace organization in that country. Israeli reservists, who were concerned when the historic peace talks with Egypt stalled, published an open letter to Prime Minister Menachem Begin urging him to continue the talks. The Israelis who supported this effort organized Peace Now, and the positive results of the Camp David peace accords with Egypt were attributed in part to the fact that Israelis were beginning to speak out and pressure their government. Over the years Peace Now has continued to support exchanging land for peace and maintains a broad-based effort to promote dialogue and understanding with Palestinians. In 1981, Americans for Peace Now was formed to provide support for Peace Now's activities and raise awareness in the United States that there are Israelis who seek peace.[2] Israelis in the peace movement urgently sought American Jewish support. They were aware that unless the United States put pressure on the Israeli government, nothing would change. To make that happen, it was necessary to break down the public perception that all American Jews supported the policies of the Israeli government. Organizations such as Americans for Peace Now continue to play an important role in that effort.

In 1980, many of the organizers of Breira decided to create another organization, New Jewish Agenda (NJA).[3] NJA had a multi-issue platform, and this mitigated, although it did not eliminate, the organized American Jewish community's harsh attacks against NJA positions. NJA's Middle East policy was still at the heart of its platform. It called for negotiation with the PLO, then controlled by Yasser Arafat's Fatah movement. The ultimate goal was achieving a two-state solution. This was still heresy in the American Jewish community.

In 1982, all that changed. Despite the peace agreement with Egypt that returned the Sinai and dismantled Israeli settlements there, the government of Israel embarked on a campaign that accelerated the building of settlements on the West Bank. When Israel invaded Lebanon, ostensibly to secure its northern border from attacks, NJA was the first organization to protest. But others in America, Israel, and the worldwide Jewish community soon joined them, no longer persuaded that the government of Israel was engaged in wars only of self-defense or the pursuit of peace.

The year 1982 also marked the beginning of Yesh Gevul (There Is a Limit), the first organized effort of reservists who went to jail instead of serving in Lebanon and who later refused to fight against the First Intifada (Palestinian uprising, 1987–1993). Other soldiers' efforts to resist have continued over the years, with Courage to Refuse groups sending letters from former combatants, pilots, and commandos in

2002–2003 and continuing to go to jail and to speak publicly against aggressive government policies.

Women have also been actively engaged in peace efforts. The most prominent organization, Women in Black, was founded during the First Intifada in 1988. A group of Jewish women began to gather at a central location in Jerusalem every Friday at noon. They dressed in black, carried signs that said "End the Occupation," and maintained a silent vigil. The vigil continues today in six Israeli cities. Inspired by the Mothers of the Plaza de Mayo in Argentina, Women in Black has in turn inspired hundreds of groups of women all over the world. Women in Black groups demonstrate not only for an end to the Israeli-Palestinian conflict but also against other wars. Women in Black is part of an umbrella group, the Coalition of Women for Peace, formed in 2000, that consists of nine Israeli feminist organizations that support an end to the occupation and peace with the Palestinians and that maintain regular communication.[4]

In response to human rights abuses by the Israeli military authorities during the Intifada, Reform, Conservative, Orthodox, and Reconstructionist rabbis formed an organization called Rabbis for Human Rights in 1988.[5] In 1989, leading Israeli intellectuals formed B'Tselem (In the Image), the Israeli Information Center for Human Rights in the Occupied Territories, to document human rights violations in the occupied territories.[6] Currently, groups such as the Israeli Committee Against Home Demolition, Birthright Unplugged, and Breaking the Silence take American Jews on tours of the West Bank so they can talk to Palestinians and ex-

amine the effects of Israeli military aggression with their
own eyes.

In part because more established groups such as Peace
Now would not support the "refuseniks," a more radical Israeli peace organization formed in 1992 called Gush Shalom
(The Peace Bloc). The peace movements received a boost
when the Oslo accords were signed in 1993, promising Israeli withdrawal from the West Bank and Gaza and the
recognition of the Palestinian Authority's right to self-rule.
When the withdrawals did not happen as planned, and when
Bill Clinton's effort at diplomacy failed, precipitating the
al-Aqsa Intifada of 2000, Gush Shalom continued to press for
peace. In recent years, they have advocated a shared capital
in Jerusalem as well as a recognition of Palestinian right of return to Israel or compensation for the lands they ceded. A list
of their actions in pursuit of peace is available on their Web
site[7] and at the online journal *Occupation Magazine.*[8]

Often Israeli peace efforts are criticized with the argument that there are no Palestinian dialogue partners. But
there have also been a number of grassroots projects that involve Israeli and Palestinian partnerships designed to foster
communication. Neve Shalom/Wahat as-Salam (Oasis of
Peace) is a village between Tel Aviv and Jerusalem where Israeli Arabs and Jews live together and conduct educational
programs. Ta'ayush is an Arab-Jewish partner group working
to end the occupation. The West-Eastern Divan, founded by
Daniel Barenboim and Edward Said, sponsors an orchestra
comprised of young Israeli and Palestinian musicians who
have played all over the world. Palestinian-Israeli Physicians

for Human Rights took Israeli doctors to the Palestinian territories to protest violations of water usage. Seeds of Peace is a summer camp that brings together Israeli, Egyptian, and Palestinian youth. The Peres Center for Peace has a "Peace Team" of Israeli and Palestinian boys who play soccer. Radio All for Peace is a joint Israeli-Palestinian radio station that broadcasts in the north of Israel and Palestine. The People's Voice is a peace agreement signed by Israeli Ami Ayalon and Palestinian Sari Nusseibeh that calls for a two-state solution with Jerusalem as an open city and the Palestinians having the right to return only to the State of Palestine.

Dialogue has also been the primary focus of some American efforts at peace. Bringing American Jews and Palestinians together to talk with one another has been an important educational strategy. Often these efforts are based on the lines of communication that were opened through Jewish-Christian dialogue. Arthur Waskow has been instrumental in organizing dialogues under the rubric "The Tent of Abraham." Waskow, along with Benedictine nun Joan Chittister and Murshid Saadi Shakur Chishti, has encouraged Jews, Christians, and Muslims to think about the ancient connections that bind us together, our common roots in the lineage of the biblical family of Abraham, and to begin our conversations from a perspective that compels us to think about how we can heal the rifts between us. Local dialogue groups that first emerged in the 1970s sponsored by mosques and synagogues continue to meet in various cities as well. Several cities now sponsor Muslim-Jewish Peace Walks, or pilgrimages for peace, that are organized by leaders of local mosques, churches, and synagogues. Walking together in silence accompanies talking together in dialogue in search of how American Jews, Christians, and Muslims can facilitate a peaceful resolution to the Palestinian-Israeli conflict. This initiative began in New Mexico and has spread to communities in Philadelphia, Los Angeles, and Las Vegas. The Tikkun community is an interfaith organization focused on conversations among religious groups with a focus on Middle East peace.

The Israeli peace movement is stronger than its American counterpart for several reasons. American Jews do not have to live in a war-torn land and can avoid thinking about Israel if they choose. As bystanders and not participants, they do not want their actions to be construed as supporting any efforts that will damage Israel, so they are particularly cautious. Because they are not Israeli or because they left Israel to live in America, they may think they must forfeit their right to speak. American Jews are also intimidated by powerful Jewish groups such as the American Israel Public Affairs Committee (AIPAC) and United Jewish Communities (UJC) that use strong repressive tactics to ensure that the voices of dissent are muted in the Jewish press. The destruction of Breira and the demise of New Jewish Agenda, along with the silencing of many of their leaders, had a chilling effect.

The 2006 war in Lebanon increased fear for Israel's safety and made public criticism more difficult. And yet organizations such as the Jewish Peace Lobby, Brit Tzedek v'Shalom (Jewish Alliance for Justice and Peace), the Israel Policy Forum, and the counterparts of various organizations

in Israel continue in their efforts for a negotiated peace and a
two-state solution. Some have been outspoken about the Israeli government's unilateral peace plan and the building of
the separation barrier that denies Palestinians access to
places outside the confines of their villages, deprives them of
work, and keeps them effectively imprisoned. Some have
made efforts to create a Jewish lobbying organization that
could rival AIPAC and exert some pressure on the U.S. government to broker a peace agreement between Israel and
the Palestinian Authority, although the breakdown in com-
munications between Hamas and Fatah (you thought only
Jews had multiple opinions?) is complicating those efforts.

American Jewish peace efforts are also divided over
strategy and philosophy. Peace organizations run by Jews
who are more closely allied with the mainstream Jewish community are convinced that a two-state solution is the only answer. They are reticent to engage with those on the Israeli
left who openly discuss post-Zionist perspectives and question whether a Jewish state should exist at all. Other American Jews, including younger ones who never knew an Israel
prior to the 1982 war in Lebanon, are open to more radical
perspectives. So are some Jewish artists and academics. Jewish Voice for Peace, an umbrella organization with groups
based in San Francisco, Philadelphia, Boston, Chicago, and
Seattle, is willing to struggle openly with questions such as
boycotts of Israeli products, divestment, and a one-state (bi-
national or secular democratic) solution. They are also willing to work with groups such as the International Solidarity
Movement.

When justice-pursuing Jews pray, they usually include their fervent wishes for peace, evoked both in the Hebrew *shalom* and the Arabic *salaam*. Peace for Israel, peace for Ishmael, peace for all the world. The work of the Jewish and Israeli groups and individuals highlighted in this chapter makes it possible to imagine those prayers are not in vain.

5

Poverty

A ccording to the Torah, "the poor will always be with us." (Deuteronomy 15:11). Judaism is a realistic religion, after all. We may harbor messianic dreams of a time of *shalom*, complete peace and prosperity. But mostly we're concerned with the realities of the world we live in, and our traditional texts don't mince words—poverty is a fact of life for much of the world's population, and, contrary to popular assumptions, also for many Jews.

The Talmud raises the question of why the world is that way. What kind of God would create poverty? The rabbis put the question in the mouth of the Roman governor Turnusrufus, who asks Rabbi Akiba: "If God loves the poor, why doesn't he take care of them?" The answer is simple: it's our job. This is what it means for us to be partners with God in creation. We are responsible for the well-being of those around us. When the Jewish community was autonomous and insular, we understood that obligation primarily as taking care of other Jews. In the global world of today, justice-seeking Jews understand that the obligation encompasses feeding "all who are hungry" as the Passover *haggadah* commands.

Jews who seek justice must confront the reality of poverty and work to ameliorate its harshness. It is our obligation to do our part so that poor people have decent lives and the basic necessities—clean air and water, food, clothing, and shelter. And while there will always be poor people, Jewish texts don't assume that poverty is a legacy passed on through the generations. It's also not a punishment or a moral category. Poverty is simply a part of God's creation and a circumstance that can happen to anyone. Our communal job is to make it less onerous. So we not only need to take care of the poor, we must also work to end the cycle of poverty that exists in our world today—to make sure the poor know how to take care of themselves. Finding ways to get poor people jobs, education, and health care is part of that plan and is what Jewish *rodfei tzedek* are most involved in doing.

The primary vehicle for combating poverty is *tzedakah*. Although it's most frequently translated as "charity," it has a different meaning in Hebrew than in English. It is not a coincidence that *tzedakah* comes from the same root as the word for justice (*tzedek*). The English word *charity* is based on compassion, derived from the Latin *caritas*, or Christian love. The equivalent in Hebrew would be *gemilut hasadim*, acts of loving kindness. Jews do those, too, in abundance. But we use the term *tzedakah* to refer to the behaviors we engage in to provide for the poor and define those actions as doing what is right. We do *tzedakah* to make the world a better place, not because poverty evokes our sympathy.

THE EIGHT RUNGS OF CHARITY

Jewish texts are concerned about feelings in relation to *tzedakah* but not the feelings of the donor. The feeling that matters is respect for the dignity of the recipient. This perspective is best illustrated in the well-known series of precepts formulated by the great twelfth-century philosopher Moses Maimonides (affectionately known as "the Rambam"). The Rambam's Eight Rungs of Charity (from the *Mishneh Torah*, "The Laws of Gifts to the Poor," 10:7–14) summarizes ancient Jewish teachings on how to give.

The highest rung is reminiscent of the oft-quoted Chinese proverb "Give a man a fish and you feed him for a day. Teach a man to fish and you feed him for a lifetime." Less eloquently but to the point, the Rambam directs us to give a gift or an interest-free loan or, better, enter into a business partnership or make sure there are jobs for those in need. The goal is not to support people but to help them become self-sufficient, which is understood to be the best way to maintain one's dignity.

The Rambam's next level enjoins giving that's anonymous on both sides so that the recipient doesn't feel shamed by the gift and the donor doesn't feel pride in his or her capacity or generosity. This secret giving was based on a tradition in which people would place donations in a box at the Temple that would then be distributed anonymously to those in need—a stark contrast to the "naming opportunities" so prevalent in fund-raising today. On the next rung down, the benefactor remains anonymous even when he or she knows to whom the gift is going. The last four levels place in descending order giving directly without being asked, giving after having been asked, giving inadequately but cheerfully, and last, giving unwillingly. Not giving is not an option.

TZEDAKAH AS COMMUNAL RESPONSIBILITY

Although Rambam's rungs speak to individual acts, *tzedakah* was a communal responsibility. Ancient laws in the book of Deuteronomy that describe the obligations of farmers in an agricultural economy set the precedent. Every Israelite who worked the land was expected to leave the corners of the field for the poor to come and harvest. The forgotten and imperfect fruit left on the trees and vines, cut stalks, and fruit scattered on the ground were not collected so that those without access to land of their own could glean food. As we will see in the chapter on the environment, land use was based on a seven-year cycle ending in the sabbatical year. In the third and sixth years of the cycle farmers were additionally obligated to tithe a portion of their harvest as *ma'aser oni*, or a tithe for the poor, instead of bringing that portion to the Temple for an offering. These ideas are predicated on the notion that humans aren't owners but stewards of the land that ultimately belongs to God. (Karl Marx may not have believed in God, but his ideas about the evils of human ownership are in keeping with this line of thinking.)

After biblical times Jews were more likely to live in urban settings in autonomous communities. The obligation to tithe agricultural bounty resulted in an understanding that Jews were obligated to tithe a percentage of their income—either one-fifth or one-tenth in a money economy. These funds permitted communities to maintain a charity fund and soup kitchen to fulfill their obligation to the poor. The community also took responsibility for providing funds for burials when the survivors couldn't afford a grave and for funding dowries so that women from poor families could marry. Physicians were expected to provide medical care even if someone couldn't afford to pay. There was also communal responsibility for primary education. The obligation to maintain education and health were so important they superseded upkeep for the synagogue and cemetery.

Jewish law set a poverty line at 200 *zuzim*, an amount that was considered enough to buy bread for a family. Although the legal discussion about basic necessities is concerned primarily with food, adequate, permanent housing was understood as a necessity. The prophets included taking people into your home (especially indigent visitors from other Jewish communities) as part of the obligation of *hachnasat orhim*, welcoming guests. This tradition continued through modern times.

Poor individuals and families assessed their own needs in relation to the definition of poverty and would help themselves from the communal funds, paying back into them what and when they could. To maintain poor people's dignity, even those who took funds were obliged to contribute. To paraphrase Marx, each member of the community could have access to what they needed but was also responsible to give back according to their ability. A scene from *Fiddler on the*

Roof illustrates this point. When the poor person asks for alms, the townsperson responds that he had a bad week, chronicling all his financial setbacks. The poor person responds, "Because you had a bad week, why should I suffer?" The humor reflects the value of interdependence of community members and the importance of giving no matter what your own circumstances might be at any time. Even the unwilling gift, the Rambam's lowest rung, is important.

Jewish values encouraged the prevention of poverty through respect for labor, captured in the Talmudic saying "Great is work, for it honors the workers." This perspective echoes biblical law (Deuteronomy 24:15 and elsewhere) that required that workers be paid promptly. This passage has been taken expansively to suggest that laborers need protection from employers who might not treat them properly.[1] The end goal of providing timely wages according to rabbinic tradition was to make sure that the laborer would be able to have the basic necessities of life and avoid poverty.

The Talmud required that every man teach his son a trade, and the stories of the rabbis in the Talmud often refer to the great variety of their occupations, from tanner to shoemaker. Although Torah study was highly valued, it was presumed that each individual would have to balance study and labor. On the Jewish holy days that begin the new year cycle, Jews pray for *parnassah*, a living wage, in the year to come, along with life's other benefits, including health and joy. The Mishnah proclaims, "No flour, no Torah"—part of the realistic approach to the necessity, and vagaries, of economic life. The sabbatical year, where debts were to be forgiven, was meant to create a society where everyone had a chance to start over again.

All this focus on providing living wages and caring for the poor when the system fails might surprise people who know Jews only by our stereotypes. Jews have, throughout our history, been characterized as more greedy than generous. I'll never forget teaching a class about Jewish death practices and explaining that it's a Jewish custom to give *tzedakah* to a charity chosen by the deceased's family instead of sending flowers. One of the students raised her hand and asked why, if giving was a Jewish value, all the Jews she knew were so cheap?

Perhaps we can blame Shakespeare's portrait of Shylock or Tevye's desire to be a rich man for this misperception. Few people know that lending money at high interest is against Jewish law, and lending that came under the rubric of *tzedakah* was required to be interest-free. Jews became involved in moneylending during the Middle Ages by circumstance, not desire. Agricultural occupations were not possible, as Jews were not permitted to be landowners in Christian societies. While many Jews were craftsmen, others developed commercial occupations. Connections with Jewish communities around the world that eased travel created opportunities for many Jews to make a living through international trade. Jewish associations with money were based on this confluence of conditions.

Looking for a scapegoat, Nazis blamed German economic problems on Jewish greed, as did their medieval predecessors, including Shakespeare and the Church. Modern anti-Semitism faulted Jews for being capitalists and communists simultaneously, and we were both. Contemporary anti-Semitic stereotypes accuse Jews of owning the banks and the media (which would be quite a shock to Rupert Murdoch and the Bank of America), and my experience traveling in Muslim countries suggests that this stereotype, although based on Jewish experience in Christian lands, is widely believed. Not surprisingly, these stereotypes don't tell the whole story. There are Jewish bankers and media moguls, but they own only a small percentage of banks and media outlets. There are Jews with wealth, but many others are part of the working poor. Some pay heed to Jewish teachings and are generous, and some are not.

TZEDAKAH TODAY

Whatever the financial circumstances or perceived attitudes others have about money and Jews, *tzedakah* is central to Jewish institutional life today. Support for Jewish organizations and for the state of Israel keeps the Jewish community vibrant. But Jews who understand the connection between *tzedek* and *tzedakah* as a requirement to step outside the Jewish community have also built institutions that are committed to a larger vision of economic justice.

Justice-seeking Jews use Jewish wealth, energy, and skills in fund-raising to work toward the broader goals of economic justice around the world. They raise money to benefit organizations that work to alleviate poverty outside the Jewish community. They are involved in coalitions that do legislative advocacy and in educational programs that teach skills and Jewish values around poverty issues. This work is often done by social action committees within synagogues. There are also a number of Jewish organizations dedicated to providing direct service and training Jewish youth to understand the value of working both inside and outside the Jewish community.

THE *TZEDAKAH* COLLECTIVE

Giving money is by far the most common way Jews practice *tzedakah* and follow Maimonidean principles. While we may frown on people who assume that giving money is all one needs to do to be a good Jew (a phenomenon known as "checkbook Judaism"), we would not be able to do what we do without the contributions people make, large and small. Some organizations collect and redistribute money. They provide the opportunity for anonymous giving, as donors give to a general fund and recipients don't know from whom they're receiving this gift.

One such organization is Ziv. In 1981 writer and poet Danny Siegel founded the Ziv Tzedakah Fund. Siegel realized that for small grassroots organizations a little seed money could go a long way. Ziv seeks out "*mitzvah* heroes" who run projects in both the Jewish and wider communities and provides them with small grants. Over the years, Ziv has distributed more than $12 million in small sums. Every year, the organization publishes an annual report that describes each of the groups that receive funding. What follows is a description of one of the organizations that illustrates what Ziv is all about:

Sunday Friends ($7,620.00)

Ziv was most fortunate when a good friend told us about Janis Baron's marvelous Sunday Friends program in San Jose, CA. It is one of the best organizations we know that allows recipients to be donors, thereby gaining a sense of empowerment and reinforcing their self-dignity. Here is a paraphrase of Janis's description of Sunday Friends: . . . On Sunday afternoons in a joyful and supportive community setting, children side-by-side with their parents and volunteers, contribute by preparing and serving healthy foods, making craft gifts for residents of nursing homes, cleaning the grounds of the facility, writing creative thank-you letters to donors, helping each other learn and more. For their contributions, they earn tickets, which they bank and later spend to "purchase" the items they want and need.[2]

The Ziv Annual Report highlights the work done by groups that might not qualify for gifts from larger organizations. In this particular case, Sunday Friends emphasizes self-sufficiency, as do many of the recipients of Ziv funding.

Mazon (Food), another organization that redistributes Jewish donations, was founded in 1985 to respond to world hunger. It not only provides funds to groups that feed the hungry but also works on systemic issues at the core of the problem. Its plan is simple and ingenious. Like the carbon offsets now used to alleviate global warming, Mazon enlists individuals (through partnerships with synagogues) who pledge to donate 3 percent of their cost when they plan weddings, *b'nai mitzvah*, and other life cycle events. Mazon contributes these funds to hunger relief organizations, such as the White Earth Land Recovery Project in Minnesota, which supports health and nutrition projects at the White Earth Indian Reservation, or Project Angel Food in Los Angeles, which delivers meals to the homebound terminally ill. As part of its advocacy program, Mazon's requirement that grantees get involved in legislative activism has stimulated a culture change in hunger relief organizations, which are often reluctant to move beyond the daily task of feeding the hungry. To encourage this change, Mazon holds a yearly conference for its California grantees that builds partnerships in the effort to seek more public funding for their programs.

LENDING: THE HIGHEST RUNG

Maimonides includes lending as part of the highest rung of *tzedakah*. Jewish Funds for Justice (JFSJ) pioneered in this aspect of Jewish giving. In addition to making grants, JFSJ developed innovative projects that encourage self-sufficiency through strategic lending. Its Tzedec program pools funding from Jewish philanthropic investors. The funds are then reinvested in community development financial institutions (CDFIs). Unlike traditional banks, these CDFIs provide no- and low-interest loans to stimulate housing, jobs, and small businesses in low- and moderate-income neighborhoods. Since its start in 1997, Tzedec has gathered over $20 million for loans in Baltimore, Washington, D.C., and Los Angeles. It also has initiatives in south Florida, Philadelphia, Boston, and the Gulf region in response to Hurricane Katrina. It lists these inspiring successes on its Web site:

- $180,000 investment in Cornerstone, Inc., has helped create safe housing and positive living situations for mentally ill residents of Washington, D.C.
- $100,000 investment in Native American Bank in Browning, Montana, has financed loans on tribal reservations across the American West.
- $200,000 investment in Los Angeles Neighborhood Housing Services has helped L.A. inner-city residents purchase their first homes.
- $100,000 investment in Latino Community Credit Union, the state's first truly bilingual banking institution, has helped serve North Carolina's growing Latino community.[3]

Since its founding in 1985, the American Jewish World Service (AJWS) has partnered with other organizations to work with communities around the globe to create and sustain economic development.[4] It has provided training to small businesses and access to credit sources. It has established relationships with groups and individuals in twenty-two countries, including the Tibetan community in exile, the Philippines, Mexico, Honduras, Haiti, Gaza, Ethiopia, Rwanda, Uganda, and El Salvador.

In El Salvador, AJWS supports Asociación Mangle, a group that maintains an agricultural microcredit program for rural, low-income families. The credit fund provides loans, training, and technical assistance on crop diversification, land preparation, organic farming, fish farming, and access to irrigation equipment. Like other AJWS programs, its goal is to create opportunities for poor people around the world to gain access to resources and obtain the skills that will allow them to live decent lives.

BEYOND GIVING AND LENDING: ACTIVISM

At the heart of Maimonides' highest rung is self-sufficiency through work. Giving and lending are critical pieces of the *tzedakah* puzzle, but making sure that people have jobs is the main way to achieve the self-sufficiency Maimonides strove for. We have seen how Jewish teaching emphasizes the need for people to support themselves. To avoid being trapped in a cycle of poverty requires that wages be at a level that allows people to meet their needs for life's basic necessities: food, clothing, shelter, health care, and education. Most Jewish anti-poverty groups are involved in improving wages and working conditions. Without decent jobs at a living wage, how can people fulfill the requirement to give *tzedakah* that was incumbent on all?

As the majority of Jews in the United States has become financially secure, and the gap between rich and poor has increased as a result of federal policies since 1980, direct involvement with or on behalf of low-income communities

poses new challenges. The most successful groups have
learned how to apply Maimonides' principle of respecting
the dignity of the poor through organizing and activism, in
addition to giving and lending. This means working to em-
power the poor to advocate on their own behalf and supporting them not only financially but politically.

WORKERS' RIGHTS

A group of Jewish organizations are involved in supporting
decent jobs at fair wages. JFSJ makes grants to organizations
such as Jobs with Justice, a coalition of labor and community
activists, students, and clergy in various regions to build al-
liances in support of low-wage workers. JFSJ supports (and
encourages you to join) a conversation about fair wages at
jspot.org.[5]

In 1990 a group of Jews in New York City, tired of the
conservative direction of Jewish priorities in that city,
founded Jews for Racial and Economic Justice (JFREJ), a
membership organization with the support of an advisory
board of close to thirty New York City rabbis. Members organize, do educational and cultural work, and get the word
out about economic justice issues through their weekly radio
program (*Beyond the Pale*), mailings, and Web site. They
have campaigned for a living wage and against sweatshops.
Their most recent initiative identifies a unique contribution
that the Jewish community can make to support domestic
workers. They joined with Domestic Workers United in
working toward state- and citywide domestic workers' bills of

rights. Through community and synagogue organizing they are building a network of employers who follow best practices regarding wages, benefits, and conditions for workers employed in their homes and who train others to do so as well. Many of their campaigns for economic justice are connected to their passion for racial justice.

Jews in America (and Russia before that) were deeply involved in the labor movement, and this legacy informs much of Jewish economic justice work. The Jewish Labor Committee (JLC) is a national organization that Yiddish unionists founded in 1934 to connect the Jewish community with the trade union movement. Its regional offices around the United States maintain a Jewish voice for workers' rights. In Philadelphia, the JLC has supported Comcast workers' right to unionize and leafleted outside Wal-Mart to protest its child labor practices. It fought Medicaid cuts in the state budget, participated in a coalition to raise the minimum wage, and demonstrated at Charles Schwab against the privatization of social security as part of a national day of action for retirement security.

The Progressive Jewish Alliance, a California-based group founded in 1999, engages Jews on issues such as prison reform and Jewish-Muslim dialogue, but its main focus has been on improving working conditions and securing a living wage for the working poor. Because of the deep historical connection between Jews and the garment industry as workers and owners, working against sweatshops has been a critical part of its agenda. It has taken a major role in the California Sweatfree coalition, which worked for ordinances in Los Angeles and San Francisco that require the garments purchased by local governments not be made in sweatshops and include funding toward enforcement and monitoring.

The lesson derived from Ziv is that small organizations and even individuals can make a difference. Rabbi Morris Allen has started his own campaign, called Hechsher Tzedek. Allen is a Conservative rabbi in Minneapolis who is working to extend the idea of kosher certification (*hechsher*) to include workers' rights at kosher packing plants. Kosher food companies hire a high proportion of Latino immigrant workers, and Allen believes they should be treated according to the highest Jewish principles regarding worker rights. He targeted AgriProcessors for paying substandard wages, doing safety training in English only, and offering only one expensive option for health care benefits. The Conservative Movement's rabbinic organization endorsed his idea, and he is developing a set of workplace standards.[6]

Workers' rights issues take up a good part of the Jewish anti-poverty agenda, but other local groups from Minnesota to Washington, D.C., have also focused on related concerns such as housing and transportation. There's no question that working on these issues also forms an important dimension of the Jewish economic justice agenda.

EDUCATING THE JEWISH COMMUNITY ABOUT POVERTY ISSUES

Jewish organizations know that they cannot continue to do this work without spreading the word and getting more Jews involved in broad-based work toward economic justice. That's why education is important. The Jewish Funds for Justice is committed to helping Jewish *rodfei tzedek* understand that social justice is not just an empty phrase in Judaism but comes straight from Jewish teachings. The JFSJ Web site provides a curriculum, teachers' guide, Torah commentaries, text studies, and articles about Jewish approaches to poverty, written by the JFSJ educational staff. These materials both educate and provide resources establishing a Jewish warrant for anti-poverty work. Jews United for Justice is at work on a guide for Jewish celebrations such as weddings and *b'nai mitzvah*, called the Simcha Project. It will encourage families to attend to labor practices in addition to donations to feed the hungry when planning such events.

For readers, *Tikkun* magazine consistently provides thoughtful and substantial articles about economic justice issues. *Zeek* and *New Voices* (and sometimes even *Heeb*) also feature articles that highlight Jewish commitments. A recent article in *New Voices* chronicled the activities and disagreements of Harvard's Progressive Jewish Alliance in support of university security guards' campaign for a fair contract, revealing that Jews who work for economic justice have more than one opinion on how to achieve it.[7]

Jewish grassroots activists have tapped the educational possibilities of the Internet. JFSJ created Jspot, where activists can engage in conversation (and let off steam). Almost 9,000 people accessed the Web site to register their preferences for a Jewish domestic agenda, demonstrating its broad reach (or the obsessive voting of a few passionate individuals). Three of the top vote getters were central to the anti-poverty agenda: wages, education, and health care. Another Web site, SocialAction.com, helps Jewish activists keep current on new and important developments about poverty issues. Alerts from organizations such as the Shalom Center and the Religious Action Center do the same.

Training is also an important educational strategy. JFSJ funds leadership workshops and training for congregations through an initiative known as Congregation-Based Community Organizing (CBCO). These activities enhance the effectiveness of synagogues engaged in local community activism that addresses systemic economic issues such as minimum wage and affordable housing initiatives. JFSJ estimates that more than eighty synagogues have joined its initiative. Matthew Kennedy, a molecular geneticist and member of Conservative congregation Tifereth Israel in Columbus, Ohio, attended the 2007 national CBCO training. Kennedy was one of thirteen Jews from five synagogues in Columbus to attend the training. He discovered that being Jewish was not only about ritual observance. He commented, "What defines me as a Jew and as a person is how I foster and nurture all of my relationships and seek to infuse each with spirituality, humanity and justice."[8]

Panim is an institute in Washington, D.C., founded nineteen years ago by Rabbi Sid Schwarz. Schwarz has dedicated his career in the rabbinate to promoting social justice. His main goal is to educate the next generation by providing advocacy and legislative training for high school students. A program called Panim el Panim (face-to-face) has trained

12,000 teens from diverse Jewish backgrounds. The training gives them an opportunity to study Jewish texts and then to apply what they learn to social activism and public policy debates. They also get to interact with experts on a range of subjects, including economic justice concerns. Another program called J-serve, an annual day of service for Jewish youth, provides service opportunities such as volunteering for food banks. J-serve also supports advocacy, including a project in Philadelphia that engaged teens in a letter-writing campaign to raise the poverty line.[9]

The many Jewish commitments to economic justice reflect Jewish values that simultaneously accept the reality of poverty and strive to limit its harshness. On the Jewish high holy days of Rosh Hashanah and Yom Kippur we don't pray only for *parnassah*, economic well-being for ourselves. We also chant an ancient prayer, *une taneh tokef*. This prayer outlines all the horrible things that can happen to us over the course of the year: fire, floods, famine, and other miseries. It reminds us that some will become richer and others poorer. The prayer recognizes that none of us is exempt from life's vagaries. But it ends on a very positive note, informing us that three things can take some of the harshness away: *teshuvah* (making amends), *tefillah* (earnest prayer), and *tzedakah*. These improve the quality of our lives and make it possible to withstand life's unpredictable harshness. *Tzedakah*, in Jewish thinking, can and does change the world.

6

The Environment

In June 2007 Jewish Funds for Justice conducted an online survey asking readers to name the top five issues they would include on a Jewish domestic agenda. The organizers did this to counteract the prevalent notion that Jews care only about Israel and foreign policy issues and don't get involved politically in what goes on domestically. Eighty-six hundred people responded to the study, and 7,149 of them included the environment among their top issues, making it the second issue after health care on the Jewish domestic agenda.[1] (Of course, there was no such unanimity beyond the first two items, lest you imagine that Jews agree overmuch about any such weighty matters.)

How did the environment become such an important issue to Jews? Was it Al Gore? Hurricane Katrina? The melting polar cap? The evangelical Christians hopping on the bandwagon? It's easy to argue that Jews, like other Americans, have become much more conscious in recent years of the dangers to the environment for which our country, and we as individuals, bear a great responsibility. But what makes environmentalism a *Jewish* issue?

The environmental movement began in the 1970s with

little connection to any religious groups. In fact, some environmental activists and thinkers saw Jewish (and Christian) traditions as part of the problem. They read the biblical creation story as a command from God for humans to master and subdue the natural world. They read Judaism as a tradition that had perpetrated anthropocentrism—a view that saw humans as the "crown of creation." On that account they held Jewish religious teachings responsible for human callousness toward the natural world that has resulted in all environmental degradation and disaster from air pollution to species endangerment.

Initially a few Jews took these criticisms to heart and began to search within Jewish teachings for resources to connect the important lessons in Jewish tradition regarding the environment to the current crisis. Some were already thinking and writing about Jewish connections to the earth, including Rabbi Everett Gendler and Roberta Kalechofsky, a novelist and animal rights activist. For Gendler, nature was central to his rural New England rabbinate. Jewish teacher, activist, and now rabbi Arthur Waskow founded the Shalom Center in order to create a Jewish response to the nuclear threat in the late 1970s, and then, seeing the connection between saving the earth from nuclear disaster and broader environmental issues, made Jewish environmentalism a key part of the organization's agenda. In 1988 Ellen Bernstein founded Shomrei Adamah (Keepers of the Earth). Bernstein describes the genesis of the organization as follows:

I found my way back to Judaism as a young person in my 20's at a time when I was seeking spiritual guidance. I was a student in the environmental studies program at U.C. Berkeley and disturbed about the rampant environmental destruction I saw everywhere around me. After exploring other traditions, I recognized I was avoiding delving into my own (having had such uninspired experiences in my youth), and that Judaism, like all enduring spiritual traditions must have the wisdom I was looking for. . . .

This was the beginning of a long journey that led me to start Shomrei Adamah, Keepers of the Earth, the first Jewish environmental organization.[2]

Waskow and Bernstein began to produce and distribute educational materials on Judaism and the environment that challenged the perception that Jewish teachings were not compatible with environmental concerns, and they put these issues on the Jewish map. But the vast majority of Jews still did not see environmentalism as a part of a Jewish agenda.

That changed dramatically in 1992 when Vice President Al Gore and Carl Sagan called together leaders of the Jewish and Christian communities for a conference that created the National Religious Partnership for the Environment. As a result, prominent leaders of Reform (Religious Action Center), Secular (National Jewish Community Relations Advisory Council, now Jewish Council for Public Affairs), and Conservative (Jewish Theological Seminary) Jewish groups

founded the Coalition on the Environment and Jewish Life
(COEJL). With strong backing from about thirty mainstream
Jewish organizations, COEJL quickly became the address
for Jewish environmental concerns. Its Web site,
www.coejl.org, provides a vast array of information that
gives depth and meaning to the Jewish commitment to
environmentalism.

What Jewish teachers and activists discovered was that
Jewish teachings could provide a blueprint for a rich environmental agenda, beginning with a rethinking of the troubling
story of creation.

RETELLING THE CREATION STORY

As we've discussed in the Introduction and Chapter 2, there
isn't only one creation story in the Bible; there are two. It's
the first creation story (Genesis 1) that's the source of early
environmentalist complaints. In it God creates humans as
the final touch, in his own image, and commands them to fill
the earth and subdue it. From this text, you could come
to the conclusion that humans are meant to dominate (and
even plunder) the resources of the earth for their own ends.
But early environmentalists should have read further. In the
second creation story (Genesis 2), humans have quite a different relationship to God's world. The name given to the
first creature, Adam, gives us a hint. The word echoes the
term *adamah*, which means "earth," the substance from
which Adam is created. So the first human is really named

"earth creature," made from the same substance as the planet and connected to it in a special way. (This pun also exists in English in the words *human* and *humus*.)

In this creation story, the earth creature is created before the garden in which it is to dwell simply as one among many phenomena, not the pinnacle of God's handiwork. When God places Adam into the garden, the instructions are to "till and watch over it." The verb for "watch over" is *shomer*, and this is the source of the name Shomrei Adamah (Keepers of the Earth). In the second telling of the creation story, humans are meant to guard and keep, to take care of the earth—that, not domination, is our job. Further, Adam is to eat only of the fruits of the trees; animals are not food. Eating anything other than fruits and vegetables is a later concession to human frailty, not the desired state in a perfect world.

Jewish environmentalism thus begins with quite a different reading of creation that makes concern for the world around us a vital part of Jewish teaching. We are stewards, not dominators, of this earth. Having reverence for the whole creation, in both versions of the story, is a critical part of what it means to be human. We can then interpret being created in the divine image in the first story in a new light. Being created in God's image as stewards of the world requires us to behave as if we are God's partners in caring for the planet. Many Jewish traditions support the notion that our actions matter in the larger scheme of things. God may be responsible in heaven, but it's up to us here on earth. The often quoted ancient *midrash* on Genesis 2 sums it up:

When God created the first human beings, God led them around the Garden of Eden and said, "Look at my works! See how beautiful they are! For your sake I created them. Do not spoil and destroy My world; for if you do, there will be no one to repair it."[3]

This reading of the creation story leads us to ask hard questions about our responsibility as humans for the well-being of the whole earth and for the myriad ways we're spoiling it. If we are truly stewards of this creation, and responsible for making sure it's neither spoiled nor destroyed, then we should be safeguarding, not plundering, our environment. This teaching has led the Jewish environmental movement to concentrate some of its advocacy efforts on global climate change. In addition to an advocacy program called Take Your Senator to Synagogue, COEJL is organizing Climate Challenge, which it describes on its Web site as:

a worldwide youth initiative to become "carbon neutral." This means educating young people about conservation and engaging them in carbon-offsetting activities such as planting shrubs and groundcover that act as mini "carbon sinks." COEJL will adapt the program for Hebrew schools, youth groups, congregations, and other communal institutions such as summer camps.[4]

They have also initiated a program called Greening Synagogues, a PowerPoint presentation available to congrega-

tions to guide them through the steps of institutional conservation. Recently, the American Jewish Committee has become involved in a renewable energy credit program to
offset its use of electricity in all its U.S. offices. The Jewish
Reconstructionist Congregation in Evanston, Illinois, will
be the first certified green synagogue in the nation. You
can follow the process on Rabbi Brant Rosen's blog at
http://shalomrav.wordpress.com/tag/green-buildings. Rosen
writes, "We're particularly proud that we are attempting to
create the first certified 'Green Synagogue' in the world.
Specifically, this means we hope to be certified at a LEED
[Leadership in Energy and Environmental Design] Gold
Level by the US Green Building Council." The Shalom Center is also giving awards to synagogues that decide to go
green; the first was won by Congregation Beth Simhat Torah,
the gay synagogue in New York.

HANUKKAH

As we saw in the chapter on war and peace, Hanukkah is a
holiday that has served Jewish needs as an antidote to Christmas and a support for those who believe that Jews should be
proud of our military exploits. But the Jewish environmental
movement has revived the ancient connection between this
holiday and the miracle of oil that was as its center for many
centuries.

One connection was initiated by COEJL and the Jewish
Council for Public Affairs. They used the first night of
Hanukkah in 2006 to begin their campaign to encourage

Jewish institutions to switch to compact fluorescent light-bulbs because they consume 75 percent less energy than standard bulbs. The organizers point out the connection to the miracle of Hanukkah—one night's oil lasted eight nights, and one compact fluorescent bulb lasts ten times as long as a comparable incandescent. Not surprisingly, given the Hanukkah connection, at least one reporter covering the story wrote that the bulbs last eight times longer.[5]

COEJL called the campaign both "a light among the nations," echoing the prophetic image of Jewish obliga-tion, and "How many Jews does it take to change a light-bulb?" reflecting the Jewish humor we've come to expect from even the most serious of justice-focused Jews. Many synagogues found this a simple way to take some respon-sibility for climate change and to make this part of a holi-day celebration. Some synagogues even went so far as to change the bulb in the Ner Tamid (the eternal light that must always be lit above the ark where the Torah scroll is kept). And the newspapers loved it. The campaign garnered pub-licity in dozens of cities, including such unlikely spots as Warren, Ohio, and Louisville, Kentucky. COEJL's Web site estimates that 50,000 bulbs sold as part of this campaign will keep 18,000 tons of carbon dioxide from entering the atmosphere.

The Shalom Center also made the link between oil and Hanukkah with a Green Menorah campaign. Accompanied by a picture of a green tree incorporating a Hanukkah lamp, the Green Menorah is a covenant, or pledge:

The Green Menorah is the symbol of a covenant among Jewish communities and congregations to renew the miracle of Hanukkah in our own generation: Using one day's oil to meet eight days' needs: doing our part so that by 2020, US oil consumption is cut by seven-eighths.[6]

Waskow is asking congregations to sign on to this pledge, which includes converting to renewable energy or buying offsets; doing an energy audit; replacing vehicles with those that have better gas mileage; walking, biking, or taking public transportation when possible; doing public policy advocacy for energy-efficient fuels and autos and for carbon taxes; and committing to the Hanukkah standard of "one day's oil for eight days' needs."[7]

TU B'SHEVAT

Tu B'Shevat is, like Hanukkah, considered a minor holiday on the Jewish calendar. Named for the day on which it is celebrated (the fifteenth day of the Hebrew month of Shevat), usually occurring in February, it was originally associated with the tithing of fruits. It was called the "new year for trees" and became a celebration that included eating fruits of different kinds (and a bit of wine drinking, too). Tu B'Shevat was a natural time to celebrate Jewish connections to nature. Ancient kabbalists had adopted the tradition of a Tu B'Shevat *seder* on the model of Passover, a time to eat and celebrate together. Some contemporary Jews began to incorporate a Tu B'Shevat *seder* into their Jewish calendar. Shomrei Adamah made the Tu B'Shevat *seder* into an environmentally centered ritual involving eating, activities, and liturgy to accompany advocacy acts to safeguard our forests and trees.

In addition to this holiday, trees have other special resonances in Jewish tradition.[8] The creation story includes the tree of knowledge of good and evil that is singled out for protection in the Garden of Eden. Our liturgy calls the Torah a "tree of life" to further echo this connection. Jewish philosopher Martin Buber speaks eloquently in his famous work *I and Thou* about the profound connection between humans and trees.

As we saw in the chapter on war and peace, there is a strong prohibition in Deuteronomy 19–20 against cutting down enemy trees during warfare:

> When in your war against a city you have to besiege it a long time in order to capture it, you must not destroy its trees, wielding the ax against them. You may eat of them, but you must not cut them down. Are trees of the field human to withdraw before you into the besieged city? Only trees that you know do not yield food may be destroyed; you may cut them down for constructing siegeworks against the city that is waging war on you, until it has been reduced.

This prohibition makes it clear how much the author of Deuteronomy valued trees as a symbol of life. Jewish environmentalists have broadened the command of *"bal tashchit"* (you must not destroy) to encompass all wasteful destruction.

There are many ways that Jews have turned our reverence for trees into action and advocacy. The COEJL Web site offers a list of fifteen (that's what the *tu* in Tu B'Shevat means) ways to conserve trees and water, including using cloth instead of paper towels, napkins, grocery bags, and lunch bags and reusing wrapping paper and junk mail. It suggests that synagogues hold paper-saving days to focus efforts on finding the right kind of recycled paper products (with over 50 percent recycled materials), including used books. (In an effort to support this strategy, consider passing this or another favorite book to a friend next Tu B'Shevat.) It also recommends political advocacy, such as sending virtual (not paper) postcards to the U.S. Forest Service to support national forests.

Tree planting is an important part of Jewish efforts to connect to the land, both in Israel and here. The Jewish National Fund began to plant trees in Palestine (later Israel) in 1928, as part of its efforts to develop agricultural settlements there. Planting trees in Israel became a very popular way to support the development of the Jewish state that resonated with Jewish values. During the Vietnam era, Jewish students were involved in an effort known as Trees for Vietnam. American Jews were asked to contribute funds to reforest areas the United States destroyed with Agent Orange. Rabbis for Human Rights embarked on a campaign, Olive Trees for Peace, to replant olive trees in Gaza and the West Bank that had been uprooted by Israeli demolition. An interfaith organization, Olive Trees Foundation for Peace, started in 2003, has a similar goal.

Others have taken even more radical steps. In 1997 a West Coast group that called itself the "Redwood Rabbis" led a Tu B'Shevat *seder* for 250 people in Headwaters Forest in California. In addition to the traditional wine, nuts, fruits, and song, this *seder* incorporated an act of civil disobedience, trespassing on private property to plant redwood sapling seeds in the forest. Although the participants were not arrested, their unique action, which tied their politics to religious observance, drew widespread attention to the problem. The Pacific Lumber Company had been logging intensively in this forest, the last unprotected old-growth redwood forest on the Pacific coast. The drastic increase in logging activities had been precipitated by a hostile takeover of the company a few years earlier. Pacific Lumber is now owned by the Maxxam Corporation, based in Houston, Texas. Charles Hurwitz, the corporation's CEO, is also a prominent member of the Jewish community in Houston. The rabbis had used other tactics to get Hurwitz's attention, including demanding that he do *teshuvah*, the act of rethinking and redressing misdeeds that Jews perform on Yom Kippur. The public demonstration at Headwater got the attention of leading environmental activists, including the Sierra Club and COEJL, who exerted further pressure on Maxxam. By 1999, Maxxam had agreed to sell 7,470 acres that were converted into a redwood reserve and to adopt logging restrictions on the rest of its property.

There is a story in the *midrash* about an old man planting

a fruit tree. A passerby asks the man why he's doing that, since he will never see its fruits. The old man replies that planting a tree is a gift for the next generation, for whom we must always be building the future. Judaism's deep connections to planting trees, ancient and modern, point toward hope for a better future for the planet.

SHABBAT AND *SHMITAH*

Connected to the concern for growing things on the earth, Judaism also teaches the human responsibility to allow the earth to rest. We are enjoined from labor on the Sabbath (from sundown Friday to sunset Saturday), and part of that obligation is also to give our world an opportunity to slow down. As Abraham Joshua Heschel taught, the Sabbath directs our attention to the deep connection between time and space. "The earth is the Lord's"; we do not own it. We are reminded that in the first creation story, the Sabbath was really the crown of creation, since humans were created on the sixth day and the Sabbath on the seventh. Jewish liturgy links Sabbath and creation, reminding us that the most creative act may be to rest and appreciate the world around us. On Shabbat we refrain from commercial activities—we give consumption a rest, too, and remind ourselves that life is about being with people who matter to us, not only about buying or doing things.

The Torah also commands us not only to rest on the seventh day but also to give the land a rest, rotating crops in the seventh year (*shmitah*), and then in the fiftieth year (seven

times seven, of course) to celebrate a jubilee (*yovel*), relin-
quishing ownership, forgiving debts, and starting over again.
Of course, we don't know whether this was ever done, nor is
the obligation meant to be carried out anywhere but in the
ancient land of Israel; it surely reads more like an ideal than a
reality that could be practiced. The biblical punishment for
not carrying this out is famine, drought, and exile from the
land. The commands of *shmitah* and *yovel* and their atten-
dant consequences are what Arthur Waskow has called "an
ecologist's warning: poison the earth, and it will poison you."[9]

These ideals encourage Jews to think about reducing
consumption, being careful about land use, and questioning
the value of acquisition of land. COEJL and the Religious Action Center have led the fight for protecting public lands such
as national parks and wildlife refuges, the lands that belong to
all the people. Given that many Jews live in the suburbs, we
should also consider other land use issues. As many others are
doing, Jewish institutions and individuals might consider re-
newing our commitment to living in smaller dwellings and in
the denser housing available in cities. We should be working
for housing policies that contain sprawl in suburban and rural
areas. And we should support local farmers' access to land by
buying locally grown foods and by opposing agribusinesses
that use vast amounts of energy to put food on our table.

NOAH

Trees and land aren't the only part of God's creation that Jewish environmentalists are concerned about. As the well-

meaning Hollywood film *Evan Almighty* illustrated, there's a very strong message in the story of Noah that supports attending to the needs of animals. We take the story of Noah and his ark for granted as a children's story of a man who built a boat, packed it with living creatures, and set off to wait out the flood. But the Noah story has a valuable lesson about the sacredness of animals from the biblical author's perspective. Each species was saved in sexual pairs for future propagation because each species is precious in its own right and has the right to survive. Humans, like Noah, are meant to save animals, not destroy them.

This perspective drives campaigns such as COEJL's efforts to preserve and protect the Endangered Species Act of 1973. The act has saved hundreds of species from extinction by protecting their habitats. But the act is constantly underfunded, and it is often threatened by legislators who want to weaken its provisions. COEJL's alerts, coordinated with the lobbying efforts of the Religious Action Center, keep this issue on the Jewish agenda.

ECO-*KASHRUT*

The Jewish principle on which compassion for animals is based is *tza'ar baalei hayyim*, which literally means "the suffering of living beings." The Bible has many laws that illustrate this principle: commanding Sabbath rest for your cattle, not yoking different kinds of animals together for plowing, not taking the young from a nest in the presence of the mother bird, and not boiling a kid in its mother's milk. Later

Jewish law prohibits hunting as sport and consequently the wearing of furs from animals that are hunted and processed in inhumane ways. Wearing fur coats—a common practice on the High Holidays, when wearing leather is prohibited by Jewish law—is also a questionable practice. Jewish teaching also cautions against animal experimentation that causes unnecessary and avoidable pain to animals without direct medical benefit to humans. Jewish tradition also insists on caring responsibly for pets.

But anyone who has ever ordered a corned beef on rye in a kosher deli or had a Jewish friend give them chicken soup for a cold can tell you that Jewish law did not place the killing of animals for food (or ritual sacrifice in biblical times) under the rubric of *tza'ar baalei hayyim.* The many laws concerning keeping kosher provide extensive instructions about which animals to eat and the correct ways to slaughter and prepare them. The only clear indication in the laws of *kashrut* of compassion for animals is in the method of slaughter called *shehitah.* Kosher slaughter requires a skilled professional using a sharp knife that cuts swiftly and horizontally across the animal's throat. The laws directly reference the principle of *tza'ar baalei hayyim* with the understanding that causing needless pain to the animal is wrong.

Like other Jewish traditions, however, *kashrut* is not static. And Jewish vegetarians think it's time for a new kind of *kashrut* that takes contemporary realities of food into account. If the principle of *tza'ar baalei hayyim* really means compassion to animals, perhaps we need to rethink the idea that eating meat is truly kosher by today's standards. Leaders of the Jewish Renewal movement coined the term "eco-*kashrut*" for a new Jewish way of attending to the values of our tradition around eating.

Eco-*kashrut* is not a new set of rules but rather a series of questions to ask ourselves about the practices governing our eating habits. Even if we decide that eating meat is an important part of our lives and central to some of our celebrations like Shabbat dinner or Passover, there are other concerns. Is it kosher to eat meat that is factory farmed—raised in conditions of intense crowding in barns, cages, stalls, or boxes in order to maximize efficiency? Is it kosher to eat animals that have become biomachines, chemically and hormonally altered to stem the diseases and disinfect the excrement that arise in factory farms? Is it kosher to eat meat from animals that have been harmed due to indifferent or lax restraining procedures, as documented in some kosher slaughterhouses? Is it kosher to eat glatt kosher meat when that procedure (which involves cutting the trachea of conscious animals) is improperly carried out? Is it kosher to eat meat prepared in factories where the workers are not paid a living wage?

Eco-*kashrut* extends beyond questions of meat eating, too. It includes what the kosher laws originally intended: a consciousness about the food we eat, where it comes from, and how we buy and prepare it. Are highly processed or heavily packaged foods kosher? Are eggs taken from a hen that hasn't had access to proper food, water, or space kosher? Is it kosher to drink milk from animals that have been medicated to improve their productivity? Are fish contaminated with mercury, caught in drag nets, or endangered by over-fishing kosher, even if they have the fins and scales that make them kosher by traditional standards? Should we eat lettuce picked by migrant workers who are exposed to toxic chemicals in the process of their work? Should we be eating or drinking from non-recycled paper or non-biodegradable plastic products?

TZEDEK, TZEDEK TIRDOF

All the ways that Jews who care about the environment have developed for caring for the earth's animal and plant life, while important, are incomplete without thinking about the impact of these issues on humans. It is obvious that we do not all bear the burdens of our polluted environment equally. Five percent of the human population uses 25 percent of the earth's resources. While not all Jews are in that 5 percent, we are disproportionately represented there. While justice for the earth, animals, and plants are absolutely necessary, Jews who pursue justice (*rodfei tzedek*) are also concerned about environmental justice for humans.

Environmental justice concerns itself with the ways environmental hazards and lack of access to environmental goods disproportionately affect women, people of color, and poor communities. They are most likely to live in areas with polluted air and water that is not safe to drink. It is not an accident that hazardous-waste sites are located in neighborhoods where poor people live and work. More often than not, it is these populations that do the (often high-risk and poorly paid) labor that provides access to consumables, both the environmentally sound and unsound. They also lack access to the kinds of choices that permit communities and individuals with wealth to live environmentally healthy lives. They are not likely to be able to afford to purchase the organic foods and hybrid cars (or even the compact fluorescents) that we claim will improve the quality of the world around us. Poor people are also most likely to live in areas that are most vulnerable to the vagaries of climate change, as many believe Hurricane Katrina and the tsunamis of the Pacific Rim have proven. And they are least likely to be able to rebuild their lives after natural disasters.

Aware of this, the Shalom Center suggests that eco-*kashrut* includes a demand for living wages for the workers in kosher packing plants and organic farms. The Religious Action Center advocates for legislation regarding the location of nuclear waste sites to protect human lives.[10] Rabbis were also involved in starting Partners for Environmental Quality in New Jersey, an organization focused on creating just and sustainable lives for all residents of that state through education and advocacy.[11] In Israel/Palestine, an organization called Bustan: Sustainable Community Action for Land and People works on environmental justice issues. *Bustan* means "fruit-yielding orchard" in both Hebrew and Arabic. Palestinians and Israelis run it cooperatively. It aims to "promote fair allocation of clean resources" and "foster a culture of sustainable self-reliance" for Arab and Jewish populations.[12]

Jewish engagement in environmental issues is broad-ranging. Jews and Jewish organizations are committed to the

full range of environmental issues, from climate change to
toxic waste control. They work on this issue based on a range
of Jewish values that demand justice for the earth and its various inhabitants. Organizations such as the Shalom Center
and the Religious Action Center do this work, but not alone.
Mainstream national Jewish organizations and a host of small
informal and interestingly named groups (such as the Jew
and the Carrot) who aren't otherwise active in Jewish communal affairs are also involved. Synagogues of all denominations and from all over the globe have found this issue
compelling and incorporated innovative programming, personal lifestyle changes for individuals, and social advocacy efforts into their lives. Environmentalism may provide the best
example of how two Jews with three opinions may work together, even when they continue to disagree.

Conclusion:
Where Do We Go from Here?

This book gives voice to the notion that pursuing justice is a central value of Torah and should guide the actions of the Jewish community. Of course, there are those who disagree. They would probably express that disagreement in two different ways. One group would argue that a focus on social justice is not an important Jewish value. The other would say that separation of church and state means religious views have no business in politics. Pragmatically, these two arguments arrive at similar conclusions: individual Jews can pursue justice all they want, but their actions have nothing to do with being Jewish.

Those who argue that social justice isn't really part of our tradition would say that it's an invention of early-twentieth-century Reform Jewish leaders who narrowed Judaism to the ethical teachings of the biblical prophets, leaving the important things, such as Jewish rituals and the Talmud, behind. Or that social justice was brought into Judaism in the late twentieth century by Jewish renewal leaders who used the ancient Hebrew liturgical phrase *"tikkun olam"* (repair of the world) to make social action more Jewishly authentic. But either way, they would say it's an illegitimate graft onto Jewish tradition. And what about *"tzedek, tzedek tirdof*," the command to pursue justice? According to this line of reasoning it meant the obligation to hire good judges, nothing more, nothing less. This perspective is well described by Steven Weiss in an online article aptly subtitled "Justice, Justice We've Never Pursued."[1] Jews' primary concerns are, in this model, to be Jewish, observe Jewish rituals, and care about Jewish survival, not to save the world.

These critics have a point. Before modern times, Jews did not have to deal with the problems we face today. After the Roman conquest in 70 C.E., Jews fought in wars only when they were conscripted into the armies of other nations. Jewish communities had clearly defined gender and sex roles, for better or worse, and had no cause for concern about race, as the category had yet to be invented. They took good care of the Jewish poor and were respectful of their land and their animals (or at least were obligated to do so by Jewish teachings) but were not expected to respond to the problems of global poverty or land use or climate change. Only the vagaries of their own poverty made them into vegetarians— what's a Sabbath dinner without chicken, after all?

But Judaism is a living tradition that has survived because we adapt to changing circumstances while continuing to connect to our past. Modern times, and especially the dramatic changes that took place in the twentieth century, have compelled Jews to think about race, the environment, gender, poverty, sexuality, and war and peace in new ways. Part of the process has been about looking more deeply into our traditional texts to find inspiration there. In this book I have sought to show how the Jewish value of pursuing justice has supported a progressive agenda, illustrated by the projects of a wide variety of Jewish groups that have taken up the challenge.

Their work is fueled by Jewish values about building a just society, providing for those who have the least among us, honoring human dignity, seeking peace. We are not concerned about whether the prophets or the authors of Torah would be appalled at what our government is doing in our name; we are appalled and we find resonance and support for our distress in their words.

All well and good, but other critics raise another important question. While they may concede that pursuing justice is a Jewish value, they are concerned that it violates a core American value, the separation of church and state. By their reasoning, a Jewish commitment to justice may motivate individual Jews to be involved in public debates, but as American citizens, not as Jews. From this point of view, all religion should stay out of politics.

The answer to why engage in social justice as Jews comes from a different understanding of church-state separation. The First Amendment includes two statements about religion. The first, the "anti-establishment" clause, says that our government is forbidden from "establishing" a religion. That means no official state church, and no favoring one religious group over another in terms of subsidy or support. The other half of the religion clause demands "free exercise" of religious freedom. No one can be told how to worship, and laws can't restrict religious beliefs or behaviors unless they are deemed contrary to the interests of society. Religious voices in public debate are not contradicted by either the anti-establishment or the religious freedom clauses in the Constitution. Separation of church and state does not mean that religious perspectives don't have a voice; it only means they don't have a veto. American democracy is built on encouraging more speech, not less. The part of the First Amendment that guarantees freedom of speech should encourage religious groups to share their perspectives in the public square.

As we well know, in the last few decades the religious right has been very vocal in its opposition to sexual and gender justice and in support of war and, until recently, rather silent on issues such as race, poverty and the environment. We should be on guard for violations of the establishment clause, such as using the pulpit (or church funds) to support candidates running for office. But rather than trying to curtail the right's right to speak, it makes more sense to join in the conversation. As we've seen, Jews have a language of moral values that is quite powerful and an obligation to speak in that language in the public arena. We cannot allow the religious right to be the only voice present.

Finally, while we can do important work as Jews, we don't have to do this alone. Other religions have moral values that should be heard in the public square. Our Jewish voice needs to be loud, clear, and distinct, and we can even have many different Jewish voices—how could we not? But they will be even louder if we join forces with the Christians, Muslims, Buddhists, Sikhs, Hindus, and Native people from their own progressive perspectives.

What is moving to me right now is that I see this coalition beginning to take shape. Evangelical Christians are beginning to make their voices heard about climate change, and Jewish organizations are working with them as part of the National Religious Partnership for the Environment. Liberal Christian religious leaders are seeking a common ground to support reproductive rights, working through the Religious Coalition for Reproductive Choice. Rabbis are creating educational materials on marriage equality as part of the Religious Institute on Sexual Morality, Justice, and Healing. Jewish scholars have participated in interfaith writing projects sponsored by the Religious Consultation on Population, Reproductive Health, and Ethics. American Jewish World Service brings a Jewish voice to interfaith coalitions working on AIDS in Africa and genocide in Darfur. Jews organize and participate in Muslim-Jewish Peace Walks for Interfaith Solidarity around the country. Jewish leaders were instrumental in organizing the Tikkun Interfaith Community and its Network of Spiritual Progressives. Rabbis also played a role in organizing Faith and Public Life: A Resource Center for Justice and the Common Good, which helps bring media attention to progressive religious grassroots efforts. I am proud that Jewish voices are part of this growing movement.

Despite our concerns, progressive Jews are becoming less reluctant to speak in a Jewish voice, a passionate and even prophetic voice, about changes that need to come about. We are recognizing that the values that compel us to oppose the widening gap between rich and poor, protest the dismantling of the safety net, work for the environment, and support debt relief for Africa, marriage equality, the rights of immigrants, prison rights, and an end to world hunger are Jewish values. They are grounded in the moral vision in our Torah that demands the pursuit of justice.

So when I find myself on a desert island with one of those quarrelsome Jews, maybe I'll just hand her this book.[2] Part of me thinks it might convince her that pursuing justice is a valid and valuable way to live as a Jew at the beginning of the twenty-first century. On the other hand, she just might start building that other synagogue for me. Either way, we'll have something fun to argue about, like two good Jews should.

Acknowledgments

About ten years ago a wonderful woman named Doris Braendel, an activist and editor at Temple University Press, came to me with a proposition. "I'm very tired of hearing about the religious right," she said. "Maybe it's time for a religious left." There was one already, I told her; it was galvanized many times in our country's history, but it just didn't have the visibility of the religious right today. "Well," Doris suggested, "maybe you should publish something about that and make it more visible." So I set about that task. The result was a collection of writings by many religious folk who were concerned about issues of social justice. The volume, *Voices of the Religious Left*, was not a bestseller. But it did provide evidence to support the notion that there is such a thing as the religious left. I owe a debt of gratitude both to Doris and to Temple University Press for urging me to do that project.

One of the authors included in that volume was a religious feminist whose writing and activism on sexual violence I admired deeply: Rita Nakashima Brock. During the past decade Rita has continued to be a major voice of the religious left, as scholar and organizer and now as editor. I'm grateful to Rita, editorial assistant Priyanka Jacob, and The New Press for this series and for the privilege of writing in it.

Today I believe even more strongly that the religious left is our best hope for changing the current political situation in the United States, and that we Jews have a strategic role to play in making this voice heard. There are so many Jewish leaders and teachers whose work is at the heart of this effort, and to whom I owe a debt of gratitude. Only a small percentage are mentioned by name in this volume. A full list of their names could go on for pages, and I would still commit crimes of omission.

Yet there are friends whose teachings have changed my life and my understanding of the pursuit of justice in such profound ways that I must thank them individually: Arthur Waskow, whose wisdom and insights lurk behind every sentence in this book; Lewis Gordon and Walter Isaac for opening my eyes to the world of Jews of color; Jeffrey Dekro and Martha Ackelsberg for teaching me about the Torah of money; Brian Walt, Mordechai Liebling, and Frances Kreimer for keeping me honest on the politics of the Middle East; Jessica Champagne and Ruth Messinger for their insights on poverty and worker justice; Nancy Fuchs Kreimer and Avi Alpert, who have made me more conscious of the environment; Judith Plaskow, Sue Elwell, Sheila Weinberg, Laura Levitt, Jacob Staub, and Linda Holtzman, my lesbian and/or feminist co-conspirators; and Janet Jakobsen, Kathleen Sands, Emilie Townes, Jennifer Butler, and Joan Martin, who are without a doubt the best allies a (not so) nice Jewish girl could have.

This book was written in a very short time frame; I can't thank Rita Brock, Christie Balka, and Avi Alpert enough for their speedy and thoughtful reading and editing.

No one should ever write a book and forget to thank her employer. I am grateful to Temple University and the faculty, staff, and students in the College of Liberal Arts, Department of Religion, and Women's Studies Program who have supported and sustained me.

No one ever writes a book and forgets to thank her family. Christie Balka and Lynn and Avi Alpert give me a long rope and remind me that I have a sense of humor, and I love them without measure.

Rebecca Alpert

August 2007

Notes

INTRODUCTION

1. As quoted (and deemed "instructive") in a review by Jim Holt, "Beyond Belief," in the *New York Times Book Review*, October 22, 2006.

2. Arik Aschermann, "Shofetim: Pursue Justice Through Mitzvot of Commission," September 8, 2005, http://rhr.israel.net/shofetim-pursue-justice-through-mitzvot-of-commission (accessed June 27, 2007).

3. Jonathan Kremer, "Justice, Pursue Justice," *Philadelphia Jewish Voice*, September 8, 2005, http://www.pjvoice.com/v4/4202justice.html (accessed June 27, 2007).

CHAPTER 1: SEXUALITY

1. Evelyn Torton Beck, ed., *Nice Jewish Girls: A Lesbian Anthology* (Watertown, MA: Persephone Press, 1982).

2. *Reconstructionist Rabbinical Association Rabbi's Manual* (Wyncote, PA: Reconstructionist Rabbinical Association, 1997), M-15.

3. Ibid., M-28.

CHAPTER 2: GENDER

1. "A Message from Reverend Carlton W. Veazey," Religious Coalition for Reproductive Choice, http://www.rcrc.org/about/index.cfm (accessed July 1, 2007).

CHAPTER 3: RACE

1. Quoted in Seth Forman, *Blacks in the Jewish Mind: A Crisis of Liberalism* (New York: NYU Press, 1998), 26.

2. See Hasia Diner, *In the Almost Promised Land: American Jews and Blacks, 1915–1935* (Westport, CT: Greenwood Press, 1977); and Cheryl Lynn Greenberg, *Troubling the Waters: Black-Jewish Relations in the American Century* (Princeton, NJ: Princeton University Press, 2006).

3. See the exhibition catalogue *Bridges and Boundaries: African Americans and American Jews*, ed. Jack Salzman with Adina Back and Gretchen Sorin (New York: George Braziller, 1992).

4. "Congregation," http://www.pbs.org/thecongregation/indepth/buildingbridges.html (accessed July 20, 2007).

5. These estimates are based on the 2004 demographic studies of the Institute for Jewish and Community Research. See Diane Tobin et al., *In Every Tongue: the Racial and Ethnic Diversity of the Jewish People* (San Francisco: Institute for Jewish and Community Research, 2005), 23.

6. www.blackjews.org (accessed July 28, 2007).

7. See its Web site, http://www.kingdomofyah.com (accessed July 31, 2007).

8. She discusses this issue at length in the chapter "Praying with Our Legs." Melanie Kaye/Kantrowitz, *The Colors of Jews: Racial Politics and Radical Diasporism* (Bloomington: Indiana University Press, 2007), 105–37.

9. Eli Faber, *Jews, Slaves and the Slave Trade: Setting the Record Straight* (New York: NYU Press, 1998).

10. Ayecha Web site, http://www.ayecha.org (accessed July 20, 2007).

11. Central Reform Congregation Web site, http://www.centralreform.org (accessed July 20, 2007).

12. Quoted in Kaye/Kantrowitz, *The Colors of Jews*, 182.

13. Ibid., 184–85.

CHAPTER 4: WAR AND PEACE

1. See "The Case of Breira" in Michael E. Staub, *Torn at the Roots: The Crisis of Jewish Liberalism in Postwar America* (New York: Columbia University Press, 2002), at http://pnews.org/Php Wiki/index.php/LimitsOfJewishDissent (accessed July 4, 2007).

2. A full description of the platform and activities are available on the Peace Now and Americans for Peace Now Web sites, http://www.peacenow.org.il/site/en/peace.asp?pi=43 and http://www.peacenow.org/about/index.asp (accessed July 4, 2007).

3. See "New Jewish Agenda: The History of an Organization, 1980–1992," a senior thesis project by Emily Nepon, http://www.newjewishagenda.org/middleeast.php (accessed July 4, 2007).

4. See its Web site, http://coalitionofwomen.org/home/english (accessed July 4, 2007).

5. See its Web site, http://rhr.israel.net/who-we-are (accessed July 4, 2007).

6. "About B'Tselem," B'Tselem Web site, http://www.btselem.org/English/About_BTselem/Index.asp (accessed July 4, 2007).

7. "List of Actions, 1992–2006," Gush Shalom Web site, http://zope.gush-shalom.org/home/en/about/1166992989 (accessed July 4, 2007).

8. http://www.kibush.co.il/ (accessed July 5, 2007).

CHAPTER 5: POVERTY

1. For further reflection on this passage, see Jill Jacobs, "The Living Wage: A Jewish Approach," *Conservative Judaism*, spring 2003, 43.

2. Ziv Annual Report, April 2007, http://www.ziv.org/ar2007/ar 2007.pdf (accessed July 16, 2007).

3. Ibid.; "Tzedec Success Stories," http://www.jewishjustice .org/jfsj.php?page=2.1.3 (accessed July 15, 2007).

4. Its mission statement reads: "American Jewish World Service (AJWS) is an international development organization motivated by Judaism's imperative to pursue justice. AJWS is dedicated to alleviating poverty, hunger and disease among the people of the developing world regardless of race, religion or nationality. Through grants to grassroots organizations, volunteer service, advocacy and education, AJWS fosters civil society, sustainable development and human rights for all people, while promoting the values and responsibilities of global citizenship within the Jewish community." American Jewish World Service Web site, http://ajws.org/index .cfm?section_id=2&sub_section_id=1 (accessed July 15, 2007).

5. You can read about other groups JFSJ funds at http:// www.jewishjustice.org/download/CurrentGrantees.pdf.

6. Samuel Freedman, "Rabbi's Campaign for Kosher Standards Expands to Include Call for Social Justice," *New York Times*, May 19, 2007.

7. Paul Katz, Abe Riesman, and Sarah Ruberman, "Harvard's Campus Activists Strike for Labor Rights Weighing in on the Tactics," *New Voices*, May 2007, http://newvoices.org/cgi-bin/article page.cgi?id=722 (accessed July 17, 2007).

8. Matthew Kennedy, "Learning About Myself at K'hilot K'doshot," *Prophetic Voices*, spring 2007, http://www.jewishjustice .org/jfsj.php?page=2.5.4.3#learning (accessed August 7, 2007).

9. See its Web site, http://www.panim.org.

CHAPTER 6: ENVIRONMENT

1. Mik Moore, "Jewish Agenda Results Are In," June 9, 2007, http://jspot.org/?p=1355 (accessed July 9, 2007).

2. Ellen Bernstein, "About Ellen," August 2005, http://www.ellenbernstein.org/about_ellen.htm (accessed July 9, 2007).

3. Ecclesiastes Rabbah, 7:28. Translated by Eilon Schwartz, "Mastery and Stewardship, Wonder and Connectedness," in *Judaism and Ecology: Created World and Revealed World*, ed. Hava Tirosh-Samuelson (Cambridge, MA: Harvard University Press for the Center for the Study of World Religions, 2002), 99.

4. "Four-Part Climate Change Campaign," Coalition on the Environment and Jewish Life Web site, http://www.coejl.org/climatechange/cc_4part.php (accessed July 9, 2007).

5. Liz Kay, "Hanukkah, Time to See the Light," *Baltimore Sun*, December 15, 2006, http://www.coejl.org/climatechange/122106clips.pdf (accessed July 10, 2007).

6. Arthur Waskow, "The Green Menorah Covenant," Shalom Center, http://www.shalomctr.org/taxonomy_menu/1/124/1 (accessed July 10, 2007).

7. Ibid.

8. For a full discussion of traditional Jewish texts on trees, see Lenn E. Goodman, "Respect for Nature in the Jewish Tradition," in *Judaism and Ecology*, 252–58.

9. Arthur Waskow, "The Shemitah and the Yovel: The Sabbatical and Jubilee Years," Shalom Center, http://www.shalomctr.org/node/295 (accessed July 10, 2007).

10. Religious Action Center, "Environmental Justice," http://rac.org/advocacy/issues/issueevj (accessed July 11, 2007).

11. Forum on Religion and Ecology, "Jewish Engaged Projects," http://environment.harvard.edu/religion/religion/judaism/projects/partners_envt.html (accessed July 11, 2007).

12. Bustan, "Vision," http://www.bustan.org/vision (accessed July 11, 2007).

CONCLUSION: WHERE DO WE GO FROM HERE?

1. Steven I. Weiss, "Is Social Justice the Soul of Judaism?" January 15, 2007, http://www.jewcy.com/dialogue/01-15/day_1_is_social_justice_the_soul_of_judaism (accessed July 29, 2007).

2. She might also benefit from reading *Righteous Indignation: A Jewish Call for Justice*, ed. Rabbi Or N. Rose, Jo Ellen Green Kaiser, and Margie Klein (Woodstock, VT: Jewish Lights Publishing, 2008).